T0163883

TEN DOORS DOWN

Robert Tickner grew up a country boy on the New South Wales mid-north coast and became an Aboriginal Legal Service lawyer and an alderman of the Sydney City Council. In 1984, he won the federal seat of Hughes, and, in 1990, he became the federal minister for Aboriginal and Torres Strait Islander affairs, in a period of great reform during the Hawke and Keating governments. He has been Australia's longest-serving minister in that role. He then became CEO of Australian Red Cross and led the organisation for a decade from 2005 to 2015.

Robert Tickner

Ten Doors Down

the story of an extraordinary adoption reunion

SCRIBE

Melbourne • London

Scribe Publications
18–20 Edward St, Brunswick, Victoria 3056, Australia

First published by Scribe 2020
Reprinted 2020

Copyright © Robert Tickner 2020

All rights reserved. Without limiting the rights under copyright reserved above, no part of this publication may be reproduced, stored in or introduced into a retrieval system, or transmitted, in any form or by any means (electronic, mechanical, photocopying, recording or otherwise) without the prior written permission of the publishers of this book.

This text includes excerpts from Kenny, P., Higgins, D., Soloff, C., & Sweid, R., *Past adoption experiences: National Research Study on the Service Response to Past Adoption Practices* (Research Report No. 21), Australian Institute of Family Studies, Melbourne, 2012.

Printed and bound in Australia by Griffin Press, part of Ovato

Scribe Publications is committed to the sustainable use of natural resources and the use of paper products made responsibly from those resources.

9781925849455 (Australian edition)
9781925938227 (e-book)

A catalogue record for this book is available from the National Library of Australia.

scribepublications.com.au

In writing this book, I expressly honour my adopted parents and my birth parents, my stepmother and stepfather, and my four wonderful sisters and brothers, who all became such a special and ongoing part of my life. And to my daughter, Jade, and son, Jack, for their contribution to the events described here. This book is dedicated to all of them.

Surplus from the sales of this book will be donated to the Justice Reform Initiative to support the growing campaign in Australia to reduce our reliance on outdated, expensive, and ineffective prisons, which will make our communities stronger and safer.

justicereforminitiative.org.au

Contents

Prologue

I have a date with destiny this Sydney summer day in late January 1993.

I have always moved fast when I'm on a mission. Today, I am truly a driven man, but, at the top of the historic sandstone stairway leading to the Royal Botanic Gardens in Sydney, just along from the Art Gallery of New South Wales, I pause to gather my thoughts.

Sydney Harbour, which Captain Arthur Phillip aptly described as 'with out exception the finest Harbour in the World', is awash with sailing boats, ferries, and pleasure craft of all kinds. Down below in the gardens, people are relaxing and enjoying the sparkle of the water, unaware of and indifferent to what is about to happen to me.

Electrified, brimming with optimism, I am catapulting down the steps into the gardens, where I soon find myself mingling with the families and couples strolling along the long arc of the stone wall that circles the harbour and leads to the Opera House. All around me are people in the Australian summer uniform of colourful shirts, dresses, shorts, and thongs. By contrast, I am dressed up for the occasion in a white shirt and casual pants. I want the person I'm meeting to know I've made an effort, but don't want to scare her with the formality of a suit. I have put a lot of thought into all aspects of today, including this simple decision of what to wear. There are so many small details to get right. I will only get one shot at this encounter and want to make it special in every way.

As I'm walking, I can't help but notice the many babies in prams and little kids with their families along the footpath. Given the nature of my fast-approaching meeting, these sightings are quite unnerving, and my edginess and anticipation of what is to come continue to mount.

When the white sails of the Opera House appear, I pull my shoulders back and stride out. I feel so strong now, I could tow a bulldozer behind me.

I run up the Opera House steps to get the best view of the surrounding area. I am early, as planned; lateness might have conveyed a lack of caring or indecision on my part, so it wasn't an option. I can see way into the distance in both directions, and I am confident that I will be able to see my rendezvous companion long before she sees me.

It's only then, looking around, that I realise the Opera House forecourt is unusually busy. Some huge and colourful carnival tents have been set up right in front of the steps, an unwelcome intrusion I hadn't anticipated when it was agreed we meet here. I hope the additional crowds won't cause any confusion. I know the person I'm soon to meet will be feeling petrified, so I want everything to run as smoothly as possible.

In the days preceding, I haven't had much time to dwell on this meeting, but now, the magnitude of it is sweeping over me. I peer into the distance trying to make out who is approaching, but my eyes are too watery to see anything properly. I realise I must be quite a sight: a 41-year-old man standing alone at the top of the Sydney Opera House steps, tears streaming down his face. Crazy thoughts spin in my head; suddenly, I see the carnival tents as a sign of our future together, full of happiness and laughter.

I pull myself together, and peer into the distance again. *Will we hug?* I wonder. *Yes, definitely. But what if she comes up behind me?* I experience a little staccato of panicked thoughts when I realise that, although we have seen photographs of each other, photographs sometimes lie. What if I don't recognise her? We have never met. I have never heard her voice.

Our scheduled meeting time is now only minutes away. I take deep breaths, and try to meditate to stabilise my roller-coaster of emotions. For some reason, my sensory awareness of everything around me is heightened. I see a solitary older woman about 400 metres away, coming from the direction of Circular Quay. Could that be her? No, a false alarm. And then another — and another. By now, my heart is in my mouth.

I see another figure even further away, but this time, I know instantly it is her. I take a photograph with the cheap throwaway camera I purchased, as an afterthought, on the way to the city this morning. Later, I will show her this photograph, and all we will be able to see is a tiny speck in the distance, barely visible. But I knew it was her, as soon as I saw her.

As the minutes tick by, the speck gradually becomes a tall handsome woman. She stops at the bottom of the crowded Opera House steps, and I bound crazily down towards her, like a man possessed. I startle a Chinese tourist standing between us as I hurtle in her direction, waving vigorously at the person just behind her. She moves out of my way just in time.

'It's me, it's me, it's me!' I shout, pointing at my chest with my fingers.

The woman looks up and sees me, and a broad smile spreads across her face.

We are swallowed up in each other's arms, weeping, laughing, and hugging in a flood of emotion.

I have met my birth mother, Maida, and she is holding her only child in her arms for the first time since the week I was born, 41 years ago.

1

Birth and adoption

I was born at 1.25 am on Christmas Eve 1951 at Crown Street Women's Hospital in Surry Hills, an inner-city suburb of Sydney on the doorstep of the central business district. Once disparagingly dismissed as a working-class slum, Surry Hills has now morphed into one of the most upmarket residential areas in Australia. Even the hospital site has been recast into a trendy residential and commercial complex, but, for many decades, it was a major maternity hospital, responsible for some of the worst practices in baby adoption in the nation.

My mother, Maida Anne Beasley, was 23 years old at the time of my birth and not married. She had grown up in the New South Wales central-west town of Orange, and had come to Sydney for my birth. As did almost all single women who became pregnant in those times, she suffered family and social pressures to leave her work, her town, and her friends. She carried the shame of her pregnancy to the city of Sydney, where she secretly gave birth to her child.

After my birth mother had signed the papers to give the child up for adoption, she was told nothing at all about where her baby had gone. The signing completed, that was the end of the matter; the law had spoken. The prevailing thinking at the time was that an adopted baby should be given a fresh beginning, free of the stigma of illegitimacy. Adopting parents were encouraged to think that the child they were taking home was unwanted by the birth mother. It took decades of campaigning for relinquishing mothers to gain public awareness and understanding of their pain.

I was given a new identity, and all doors were firmly shut between my birth mother, my wider family, and me until the law changed in New South Wales some 40 years later. Being a sensitive, kind, and loving person, my adoptive mother, Gwen, must have given some thought to what my birth mother would have been feeling, but, in those days, no contact with an adopted child's birth mother was possible. The whole process was shrouded in confidentiality and secrecy.

The Adoption Order of the Supreme Court of New South Wales is a formal, legalistic document. Mine began 'In the matter of David John Beasley (to be known as Robert Edward Tickner) in the matter of the Child Welfare Act 1939, Part XIX' and was dated Thursday 24 April 1952, almost four months after my new mother and father 'took delivery' of me in December 1951. The final adoption order was made by Judge Dovey of the New South Wales Supreme Court, who became better known to many Australians in later years as the father of Margaret Whitlam, wife of prime minister Gough Whitlam. It notes various affidavits of departmental officials and those of Bertie Robert Tickner and Gwendoline Daisy Tickner, my new parents.

Gwen and Bert took me from the hospital to Gwen's mother's house at 18 Lansdowne Street, Merrylands, a suburb of western Sydney. Without a doubt, I was a very welcome addition to the family. My mother and father were both in their early forties and, despite marrying in their twenties, had not been able to have any children of their own. This wasn't something my parents ever discussed with me, but, as a child, I came to piece it together through fragments of overheard conversations. I don't know why they hadn't been able to conceive, and perhaps they didn't know themselves, given the limitations of medical science at the time, but their strong desire for a child was certainly why they turned to adoption.

To say I was showered with love by my mother and father is a massive understatement. When I look at the photographs of Gwen, my mother, gazing besottedly at her tiny new baby, and later her young child, I can feel the love emanating from them. I often think about what it must have been like for her in those early days of my life, as it's plain to see she must have wanted a child so much. I vividly remember her saying to me often as she got older, 'I cannot imagine my life without you. Your arrival completely transformed my life.'

At the time of my adoption, my mother and father were living in Forster, a sleepy seaside town some 300 kilometres north of Sydney. They'd moved there in 1949 with the intention of semi-retiring, or at least adopting a slower pace of life, even though they were not yet 40 years old. They had met in their late teens through my dad's younger sister,

Dorrie, who was a tennis-playing partner of my mother, and, within a few years, they had married at St John's Anglican Cathedral in Parramatta.

Forster and its twin town of Tuncurry were little more than tiny fishing villages in the 1950s, with a bridge yet to be built across Wallis Lake. The only access was via a punt operated by the Blows family. I guess, on reflection, my mother and father were very early pioneers of the sea-change movement, in that they left a prosperous city business — a sporting goods and piano store in Parramatta — to take up a new life in this small seaside spot with a combined population of approximately 1,500–2,000 people. Dad had ideas of living a semiretired fishing life and operating a boatshed as a hobby, which he did in his early years in Forster. My parents had been the mixed doubles tennis champions of Western Sydney before they moved to Forster, and had planned to play more tennis in their new country home, but they were unable to find many people to play with in this little coastal fishing village.

They lived in a white two-storey weatherboard home at 14 Lake Street, inadvertently located directly opposite both the Forster Catholic church and the local masonic lodge. It must have been one of just a handful of two-storey houses in the town at that time, and it still stands, but has been moved forward on the block and become part of the Ingleburn RSL holiday units. The house was built not long before I arrived in Forster, and, now I think about it, the second upstairs bedroom was probably waiting for the arrival of the new baby.

There was a huge backyard, with a cottage at the rear that my parents rented out, when it wasn't being used by visiting friends and family. Also at the back of the house was a huge tiered stand supporting a giant tank. The tank supplied our household water as there was no proper town water supply at that time. Down the path was the pan toilet, and, in the early years, the nightsoil cans were hand-collected by a heroic and dedicated council workforce. From those years as a small boy, I can still remember the stench of those collection days!

We lived in the heart of town, four blocks from the local ocean pool, two-and-a-bit blocks from my beloved Pebbly Beach and the lake, and about seven blocks from the local high school. I walked, and later rode my bike, everywhere, often not bothering to wear shoes unless reminded. It was the perfect place for a child to grow up. I felt I knew pretty much everyone in the town and certainly greeted anyone I saw on the street in a warm and friendly manner. My childhood in Forster was idyllic in many ways. My parents were quite strict, but, whenever I return to my earliest memories, I can only evoke the swelling pride and love they showed me. For my mother, in the fortieth year of her life, I was a gift from heaven.

Even in their early years in Forster, my parents were highly respected people. They must also have been the talk of the town with their sudden new baby. In a small country town, where everybody knew everybody, there were few secrets, and the fact that I was adopted was never hidden from me. Ever since I can remember, I have always known and never had the slightest concern about it. My mother told me I was 'chosen' by her and my dad, and that was good enough for me as a child. I believed it without question. As my parents intended, I got the feeling I was lucky, because, while other kids just were born to their parents, my mum and dad chose the child they wanted. I felt greatly loved and appreciated as their child, which is what most of us want. This I truly believe. For a child, being and feeling loved is one of the bedrocks on which their future life is built.

I do remember one occasion, probably when I was about ten, when there was a fleeting conversation with my mum about my adoption, and she proffered some very basic information about my birth parents, although she didn't refer to them as that. The name 'Beasley' was mentioned, and something was said about electricity or electrical engineering. Clearly in my own mind I didn't need any more information at that time, as I was growing up with such a loving and supportive mum and dad.

For my part, I was fiercely proud of my adoption. All my mates knew I was adopted, and I can't recall it being mentioned much by any of them, if at all — or at least not that I was aware of. In my early years of high school, I did once think I heard a classmate say something derogatory about my adoption. I know now that I completely misunderstood the incident, but at the time I became so upset and furious that I refused to talk to him for a long time, which was some feat in a class of about 30 kids who saw each other almost daily. We eventually patched things up and remain close mates.

I had asthma as a small child, so my parents encouraged me to take up competitive swimming at the age of six as a way of building my lung capacity. My father took on the role of coaching me, along with dozens of local kids. He approached the task in a very scientific way, reading widely and attending coaching clinics conducted by Forbes Carlile in Sydney. Perhaps he needed all the help he could get as he couldn't swim a stroke himself! The main training pool was Forster ocean baths, a 50-metre saltwater pool, and I could ride there on my bike in five minutes. It still gives me the horrors when I remember diving into the often chilly water, especially as winter approached. As a tall scrawny kid without an ounce of fat, I was particularly vulnerable to the cold. I always aimed to swim in Lane 6, closest to the wall, rather than Lane 1, which was exposed to the vast icy expanse of the main pool and was like being banished to Siberia. On the other hand, in the summer, when fresh water might not wash in from the ocean for weeks on end, the pollution in the pool could become intolerable.

Dad decided to build a large, 12.5-metre fibreglass swimming pool at his Forster factory, which was then installed in our backyard, much to my mother's consternation. It was a massive intrusion into the garden she loved so much and had built up over the years. The local swim squad took up what seemed like permanent residence in our backyard heated pool during the winter months, and it was also a year-long attraction for the local kids, including my friends. Despite her initial misgivings, Mum enjoyed looking out her kitchen window directly onto dozens of kids in the pool, and my dad pacing up and down the side with his stopwatch. I was especially happy to have such a honey pot of attraction for my mates in our backyard.

As a young boy, I was adventurous. I got up to things that would never be allowed these days, including designing and digging a vast underground tunnelling project in the backyard. My engineering feats would extend for three or four metres under the sand, which in hindsight I can allow was probably particularly dangerous. Mum and Dad warned me about this, but I persisted until they finally banned the practice. I also became obsessed with devising ways to bring down massive branches of the huge gum trees in our backyard, using ropes and the brute strength of my gang of nature-marauding mates. Today, I am horrified by my mindless path of destruction, which was briefly added to when I was given an air rifle when I was about ten. I managed to shoot a small bird with the rifle, but then instantly became so mortified and ashamed of my actions that I never used the gun again.

Tim, my dog, was my constant companion and friend and followed me everywhere. He was part kelpie, and a more devoted and loving pal I couldn't have wished to have. With no brothers and sisters of my own, perhaps, for me, he filled that void. He was a huge part of my life until my seventeenth year, when he finally had to be put down due to injuries and very old age. We buried him in the backyard; I remember that burial spot to this day.

Our small family of three was harmonious, and our household was free of conflict for all my childhood years. Even though there was no one to compete with me for my parents' time and affection, this doesn't mean that I was spoilt or showered with material possessions. On the contrary, because my parents were much older than those of most of my friends, they were rather conservative in their parenting. In my teenage years, I often found myself more confined in what I could do than my contemporaries — and because we lived in a small town where everyone knew everyone else, I didn't have the cover of a big city to get up to mischief.

Growing up without brothers and sisters in a very peaceful home environment arguably had its downside, too, as I later realised. Living a very protected life in lots of ways meant I didn't learn how to deal with conflict until much later in life. Even now, I don't do conflict well, which is perhaps a strange admission from someone who spent 18 years as an elected representative! I was close friends with Terry Sanders, the daughter of our local doctor, Gordon Sanders, and, in contrast to my own home life, whenever I visited her house, I was astounded by her and her brothers' robust and voluble relationship. The shouting and banter of her two brothers, Don and Peter, provided a background noise I wasn't used to, and I was often intimidated by the chaos of their house.

Occasionally as a child, I thought about what I would do if I didn't have my mum and dad to look after me. Although I was very close to all my aunties and uncles, they were mostly older than my parents and living far away from Forster — my beloved hometown, which I never wanted to leave. Doctor Sanders had been our long-term family physician, and I decided that if anything happened to my parents, the Sanders family would take me in, even though I didn't have any real basis for this conclusion.

Of course, this question of what would happen to me was probably in the back of Mum and Dad's minds as well. My bond with them was all-embracing, and they must have been conscious of how very dependent I was on them. There was no one in the wider family who could easily look after me if anything happened to them.

2

Father Bert and Mother Gwen

At every level, my mother and father were a well-suited couple. They fitted together and complemented each other in so many ways. By any measure, they were a handsome couple, but, much more importantly, they were outstanding people with an obvious integrity about them.

Born in 1910 in the tiny town of Tallong, near Goulburn, New South Wales, where his family ran an orchard, my father, Bert, was a strong, lean man due to a lifetime of hard work and active participation in sport. His family were very strong cricketers in the region, and I have a photograph of the Tickner family cricket team, which played the Goulburn team in a match in 1919 and won. The tiny stone house where Bert and his siblings grew up is still standing, but the orchard has long gone. Mum and Dad named me Robert Edward Tickner after my father's father, who passed away before I was born. As a small boy, I saw a photograph of his headstone and was unnerved to see my own name on a grave.

The Tickner family left the Goulburn region and moved to western Sydney, and, having left school at the age of 13, my father went to work. Six years later, when the Depression hit and he lost his job, he went door-to-door selling. Even in those dark years, he displayed the entrepreneurial and resilient spirit that would hugely shape my own life.

My father rarely wore a suit except for major public occasions. He wore long pants and long-sleeved shirts almost all the time, usually supplemented with a hat in the summer. My own conservative fashion sense is cast in his image — I continue to dress this way to this day, unless I'm compelled to dress up. When my father did wear a suit, he wore it well, and, when sometimes I tagged along on trips to Sydney, I could see he was quite at home in that milieu, negotiating challenging business deals.

My father spoke well, with an appealing voice honed through a lifetime of entrepreneurial business activities. He could tell a good story, but he wasn't a showy person; if anything, he was a little shy. He could hold his own with anyone in a one-on-one conversation or in a small group, but he absolutely loathed public speaking and would go out of his way to avoid it. I saw him as ruggedly handsome, in his own way, and he was always tanned from all the time he spent in the sun. He was also a reasonably tall man, being just over six feet.

On weekends, my father played golf on Saturdays, and he and Mum would usually play together each Sunday, with me tagging along. I learnt to play myself and joined them on the course as soon as I was old enough. Early on in my parents' time in Forster, my father played the leading role in building the Forster-Tuncurry golf course at One Mile Beach. He worked with key supporters to secure the land from the state government, then he got on a tractor and, with a handful of locals, physically built the first nine holes of the course, which still stand today. Both he and Mum were later honoured with life membership of the Forster Tuncurry Golf Club.

My father was from a very different generation of Australians, and one consequence of that was that he didn't easily or demonstrably show his feelings to either my mother or me, especially once I grew into an adolescent. Nevertheless, he was deeply devoted to Mum and respected her with almost a reverence — something he also instilled in me. They rarely argued, and life at home was very peaceful. I remember a loving childhood with him, and vividly recall sitting on his knee on one of our old plush lounge-room chairs, plucking his whiskers. Throughout most of my childhood, my father worked very long hours and was running two substantial businesses, one in Forster and the other in the town of Taree, 40 kilometres away. Even so, besides taking on the role of local swimming coach most mornings and afternoons throughout the year, in summer he and Mum would drive me to swimming carnivals up and down the New South Wales mid-north coast.

Dad and I also spent a lot of time together through his driving me to school. Despite this, I don't recall him ever talking to me about my adoption. The very few conversations I had about it were initiated by my mother.

I do, however, recall my father as being the parent who administered the discipline. I was mostly a well-behaved child, but there were times when I no doubt deserved the 'switch'—a relatively spindly piece of the New Zealand Christmas bush that grew at the front of our house. When I was about six or seven, on one of those rare occasions when he came after me with the switch, he chased me around the house to hit me with it, only to realise, as he chased me around their bed, that I was now outpacing him. Laughter broke through his stern veneer, the punishment dissolved into a joke, and the chase was abandoned.

From a young age, I liked to play practical jokes on my father. When I was about six years old, one of these jokes backfired and ended in disaster and destruction. Our toilet was located well down the backyard, with a key to lock the door. As an inquisitive small child, I'd discovered that the key could be used on the outside of the door to lock in any unsuspecting adult, condemning them to a period of captivity in the company of the stinking pan toilet. One morning, just before going off to school, I snuck up on my dad and silently turned the key, which I had earlier shifted to the outside of the door. Unfortunately, after I'd tiptoed back to the house I got distracted and forgot that I'd locked him in there. I skipped off to school, saying goodbye to my mother, who was working in the garden at the front of the house. Only some considerable time later did she hear a faint noise in the distance, which sounded suspiciously like someone was trying to demolish part of our house. Indeed, my father, having failed for half an hour to attract my mother's attention with his yelling, had kicked his way out of the toilet, demolishing the door in the process.

I came home from school in the afternoon while he was still at work and was bewildered to find the toilet door smashed to bits. My father never mentioned the incident to me, and it was left to my mother to explain what had happened. I sheepishly said, 'Sorry about the door, Dad,' but received only a perfunctory grunt in reply. But my father's wry smile whenever the topic was raised in later years by friends or family suggested that he came to see the humour in it down the track.

By the time I was in primary school, my father's businesses were going gangbusters. In 1957, he had launched Mid North Coast Moulded Products, a fibreglass-manufacturing business in Forster that manufactured the Sunliner caravans. My mother worked in the office in the early days. Dad carried on this business for eight years until the costs of manufacturing in country New South Wales finally got the better of him. There were over 500 vans produced, most of which are still on the road, and they have become an Australian icon. Ultimately, Dad lost a lot of money in the venture, but gave it all he had to make it a success. His work in building up the factory showed what an entrepreneur he was, which was all the more extraordinary as he had had little formal education.

Almost to prove our family commitment to caravanning, we undertook marathon treks, including all the way to Cairns twice, on very narrow and dusty roads. Of course, it may also have been partly to do with my father's fear of flying. It was torturous long-distance confinement to me as a boy, but nowadays I get a kick out of seeing these

Sunliner caravans on the road, 60 years after they were first built in Forster by my dad and his dedicated workforce. I often go out of my way to talk to the owners, who are all Sunliner devotees and thrilled to learn something of the history of their van. In September 2018, I was honoured to be invited back to Forster-Tuncurry, not in my own right, but as 'Bert Tickner's son' for a sixtieth-birthday celebration of Sunliner caravans. I could not believe the respect, and even reverence, in which my father was held by the large number of devoted Sunliner caravan owners gathered in Tuncurry for this event. My father's signature, so familiar to me, was proudly displayed on the windows of numerous vans, alongside the history of the caravan factory in Forster. As a humble person, he would have been deeply touched to be so remembered.

My father's second business was a major car dealership in the nearby town of Taree called Mid North Coast Motors. He sold Volkswagens in their 1950s and 1960s heyday, as well as Land Rovers and Rovers to the farmers and graziers of the region. I remember him telling me that the Hollywood actor Anne Baxter (granddaughter of the famed architect Frank Lloyd Wright) once purchased a Land Rover from him.

Being the son of a car dealer had its upsides: we always had interesting cars in the driveway. I learnt to drive in about 15 different cars, as they were recycled from the car lot to our home and then back to the business. I quite liked the fact that Dad sometimes drove high-performance or exotic cars, and one I especially liked at the time was the Fiat 124 Sports Coupé. In Year 11 at high school, before I got my licence,

Dad would drive me in one of these vehicles from Forster to Taree and drop me off. Although I was getting dropped off in a flash-looking car, I would invariably be late for my maths class — although that was due to me being slow to get ready and certainly nothing to do with Dad's driving, which sometimes pushed the boundaries before speed cameras and common sense prevailed.

In addition to running his two businesses full-time, my father also invented things in a backyard shed that was more like a small factory. Here, various innovative water pumps were developed, along with contraptions to better manage drainage and water circulation around the house, and refinements to improve the performance of his motor cars. It all left me in complete awe. I remember watching his weird, electrically powered pool-cleaning contraption, made from old washing-machine parts, cleaning the walls of the pool while at the same time slowly propelling itself on wheels along the edge of the pool. Phenomenal. I had some self-interest in this particular invention because, if successful, it would relieve me of my pool-cleaning duties. Alas, ultimately that wasn't the case, as some technical problems could not be overcome.

Sadly, in spite of all of my father's early encouragement to do with practical skills, I've never had a shed in my life, and my workshop skills are an absolute disgrace. If there was one thing that was guaranteed to make my father very angry, it was when I thoughtlessly 'borrowed' one of his tools, like a hammer or precious drill, and left it outside in the weather for days.

Our relationship changed a little in my later teenage years, as I think it does in most homes. I was never particularly rebellious, but, like all teenagers, I needed to find my own place in the world. We clashed during those few years when I was staking out my increasing independence, mainly because he wanted me to work more around the house and yard, and I wanted to go surfing.

From the age of 14, I was became a very committed surfer, and this represented another world to my father — one he wasn't comfortable with. Even before I took up surfing, I was aware that it was competition for the swimming club, and that my father didn't think highly of surfers. But the lure of the ocean was hard to resist: often there would be fantastic surf only a couple of hundred metres away, over the back wall of the ocean baths. Swimming training never stood a chance faced with competition like that.

I became fanatically devoted to surfing and a love of the ocean, and even studied for my school and later my university law exams on Pebbly Beach. I knew this stony beach like the back of my hand, and I surfed as radically as I could, as a local kid with inside knowledge of its hard break right onto the oyster-encrusted rocks. Often, my mates and I ended up with deep oyster cuts on our backs when we fell off our boards, and, in hindsight, it's a wonder that we didn't suffer serious spinal damage. I was never around to perform the chores Dad wanted; I'm sure he thought, during that period, that I was destined to be a beach bum.

Whatever stresses my father and I imposed on each other during my adolescence, I never had any trouble showing affection to my mother, and it is my relationship with her that most affected my later thinking about the relative influence of nature and nurture in shaping my identity.

My mother was born Gwendoline Daisy Osborn. She both came into the world and grew up in the house at 18 Lansdowne Street, Merrylands, where I was taken to meet my grandmother immediately after my adoption. The house was likely constructed in the late 1800s, and still stands, although it was substantially altered in about 2005 and looks quite different now from my childhood memory of it. Mum's father, David Osborn, worked at the Clyde Engineering Works and passed away before I was born. Her mother, Minnie Osborn, and the Lansdowne Street house were both to play a large part in my life. My Grandma Osborn was a direct descendant of Andrew Fishburn, a carpenter on the First Fleet. Andrew Fishburn travelled for part of the journey on the flagship *Sirius*, where he undertook repairs, but he arrived in Sydney in 1788 on the *Alexander*. He came from Whitby in North Yorkshire, where the ship that would later be called the *Endeavour* and be captained by James Cook, had been built by the Fishburn family shipbuilders. Research continues on Andrew's relationship to that English Fishburn family.

There were five daughters growing up in the Lansdowne Street house: Elsa, Alma, Gladys, Daphne, and my mother, Gwen, the youngest. Another sister, Marjorie, had passed away as a child. Gladys died before I was born, but the surviving sisters were an impressive quartet of strong and competent women, who kept a strong family bond throughout their lives. They all had warm and engaging personalities, and I became very close to each of them.

My mother was a slim and attractive woman, five foot three inches tall, with a broad and welcoming smile. Her skin was forever bronzed by the Forster sun, and provided a warm contrast to her hair, which turned white quite early in her life. She was a very fit woman and, after her years as a champion tennis player in western Sydney, on moving to Forster, she became a successful golfer. My mother spoke in gentle tones and had an easy self-confidence that allowed her to mix well with people from all walks of life. She was an extremely down-to-earth woman and very strong and self-reliant in so many ways. She dressed stylishly, buying some of her clothes by catalogue order from David Jones, and her hair was always fashionably groomed.

My mother was central to my life. Although she supported my father in the family businesses, she was very much focused on being my mum, and we spent a huge amount of time together when I was a small child, and later, when I took up competitive swimming. Mum would do anything for me and my mates as we were growing up, from piling our surfboards on top of her car and driving along some near inaccessible sandy track to reach the beach, to collecting us all after we missed the bus as 17-year-olds on our first day at Taree High School. Much to my embarrassment on that occasion, Mum chased the bus in her car, eventually caught it halfway, and we had to troop on board.

I think my mother largely shared my father's conservative political views in the early days, but her way of relating to people was very special. She was respected by all because she treated others with respect, whatever their background or role in life, and while she might sometimes have appeared a little distant, no one could fail to see her kindness towards everyone she dealt with. She certainly never shared my father's prejudiced views about Aboriginal people, and encouraged me to be on good terms with the Aboriginal kids in my school and their families in the town.

My mother instilled the values of fairness and kindness in me from my earliest years, and the thought that I might see myself as better than others would have been anathema to her. Because of her, I have always detested elitist, arrogant, or bullying behaviour, and since early high school I've also had a strong commitment to social justice and humanitarian values. I still have the passionate article I wrote for the school magazine when I was 18, in which I champion humanitarian principles and express concern about the threat of nuclear weapons to the people of the world.

Before my adoption reunion, I believed it was the huge influence of my mother on me, her nurturing, which created the humanitarian values that I regard as the very essence of my being. And I believed that it was my father's influence that contributed to my high energy levels, strong conscience, and commitment to try to make the world a better place. The future was to reveal that life was far more complex indeed.

3

Leaving the nest

For kindergarten and primary school, I attended Forster Central School — a small local-district school only five doors away from our house in Lake Street. The primary school was tiny, with only about 30 kids in my entire year, so we were a close-knit group. I grew up relating to kids who lived very different lives to me, including the Aboriginal kids in my class. Almost all of them lived on the 'Aboriginal Reserve'. They were mostly from the Worimi people, whose lands included the Great Lakes regions and extended right down to Port Stephens.

Once I'd finished primary school, Forster High School was a ten-minute bike ride from home, and fronted the ocean. It only went up to Year 10, but I spent four wonderful years there. During those years in our little country school, I loved my studies, my friends, and my sports, and I was honoured to be made school captain.

Mum and Dad always encouraged me to study, although they'd left school early themselves, as many of their generation had done. I did relatively well, partly because of their encouragement, but also due to my own self-motivation and a degree of competitiveness. This competitive streak probably developed as a response to being beaten by a succession of girls in my class, starting in primary school with my friend Terry, who still taunts me about it now. Maths was never a strength for me, but my greatest weaknesses were spelling and handwriting. In all my academic life, I only ever failed one subject, and it was spelling-related. My teachers accused me of using my appalling writing to cover up my bad spelling, but it wasn't deliberate — at least not until they suggested it. I realised how helpful this trick could be, and in later life I perfected the technique so as to cover up my occasional embarrassment when it came to trying to spell a word I didn't know. I also frequently reversed numbers, which led me to wonder at times whether I might be mildly dyslexic. Perhaps this is the reason that much of my life's work has involved talking for a living!

One of my favourite subjects was history, both in primary school and at high school, although in hindsight I can see that my classmates and I were poorly served by the curriculum of the day. That curriculum focused on English kings and queens, and had a very limited treatment of Australian history: I wasn't taught one jot about anything to do with the history of Aboriginal people in my area or their rich cultural history as representatives of the First Australians. I still have on my shelf the official New South Wales school history textbook from 1967 — my Year 10 Higher School Certificate year and, more importantly, the historic year of the referendum recognising Aboriginal citizenship and approving the expansion of the Commonwealth government's role in Aboriginal affairs. This government-issued textbook is almost criminal in its content, purveying the most awful, prejudiced views to young minds. It describes Aboriginal people as a 'problem' due to their loss of 'the high moral and ethical traits of their ancestors' and because they had 'also failed to accept the white man's moral and legal codes'. They were 'lazy individuals, apparently devoid of morals, and always prepared to lie, cheat or steal'. By the time we got to Year 10, most of my Aboriginal classmates had sadly dropped out of school, but for the few who remained, this book must have been excruciating. How repugnant to read such a grossly unfounded and shocking description of themselves and their families.

Whole generations of Australian schoolkids were subjected to this appalling and inaccurate portrayal of the First Australians. A little over 23 years later, after I became the minister for Aboriginal and Torres Strait Islander affairs in 1990, I would launch the National Reconciliation and Schooling Strategy to ensure that all Australian students would have the opportunity to learn the true history of our country, and about Aboriginal and Torres Strait Islander history and culture, which is such a great gift to all of us.

My parents weren't wealthy, but would have been best described as comfortably middle class, living a quiet and modest lifestyle. Nevertheless, they wanted to send me to The King's School in Sydney — first when I finished primary school, and then again when I finished at Forster

High School and needed to find somewhere else for Years 11 and 12. In fact, they told me that they'd booked my place. The thought of going away to boarding school was miserable to me, and I was adamant that I didn't want to go. To this day, I am so pleased that I resisted, and I'm even happier that my will was allowed to prevail. Growing up as a country kid and attending local schools was one of the great experiences of my life, although I only truly recognised this in hindsight.

Taree High was a much larger school, and, although I was chuffed to be made vice-captain not long after arriving there, at first I found it hard and felt like a Forster-fish out of water. Some of the teachers looked upon — or should I say, looked down upon — us Forster kids as interlopers who brought the subversive surfing culture to the school. I was caught up in that perception in the beginning and had to fight my way past it to undertake higher levels in my chosen subjects for the Higher School Certificate.

I will admit there may have been some validity to the teachers' paranoia about an insidious Forster surfing culture. I vividly remember sitting in English classes at Forster High beside a surfboard-riding buddy, Robert Willis, and giving every impression of paying rapturous attention to our English teacher, Mr Dark, as he delivered his lesson. In fact, Robert and I had developed a creative technique of imagining that the wall behind Mr Dark was a breaking wave. Every English class we rode that wave in our minds, which we could easily do for the entire length of the class. It certainly made Chaucer much more interesting.

I did well in my Year 12 Higher School Certificate, and the time came to choose a future career direction. I had no idea what I wanted to do with my life, but I knew I had an interest in politics. Aged 18, I was aware of the damage that governments could do, as well as their capacity to do good and help build a better world. Although my views at the time were relatively unformed, I confided to a trusted friend that one day I wanted to be prime minister. No one could accuse me of not being ambitious!

Whatever I was to become, I had no choice but to leave home if I was going to pursue university study. At first I thought I could do good in the world by studying medicine, and I explored this possibility in an inconclusive conversation with Dr Sanders. But in the end, my loathing of mathematics and chemistry put me off the medical path. At Taree High, I had enjoyed debating and had won the declamation competition; this made me feel confident that I would make a good advocate, and so I chose to study law. That choice meant there was only one university to go to — Sydney — as there was no other law school in the state at that time.

I didn't have any family I could stay with long-term in Sydney, and none of my close friends from Forster were heading there, so sharing a house wasn't an option. Instead, I was encouraged by my Taree High School English teacher, Mrs Willis, to consider living at St Paul's College within the University of Sydney, where her sons had also lived. On her recommendation, Mum and Dad took me to meet the college warden, Reverend Bennie, for an interview. At the start of 1970, I took up a place in the college after a few short weeks of interim accommodation with my Aunty Dorrie, my father's younger sister, and her husband, my Uncle Les, who also happened to live in Merrylands — the same suburb where my mother's mother lived.

The sandstone college of St Paul's was founded in 1856 and is Australia's oldest university college. I found it to be a blokey place, with an elite private-school-oriented culture. In 1973, I attended a college dinner where Prime Minister Gough Whitlam, a former college resident, returned as a guest speaker. As part of his speech, he said to the assembled college fraternity in his imperious and lofty tones, 'Your fathers helped shape my political views.' It was a barbed comment I could resoundingly endorse, adding under my breath, 'As their sons did mine.'

In my day, well over 90 per cent of the college residents came from the most exclusive non-Catholic private schools. Coming from a country government school as I did, I found many of the other residents wanted nothing to do with me. Walking back from the college library to my room late at night along the cold sandstone corridors, I would often pass someone going the other direction and offer a 'Hi, mate' as an opener. Usually, the response was silence or at most a perfunctory grunt. This was an experience shared by others from state schools. To be fair, it could also have had something to do with the 'fresher system', wherein first-year students were treated contemptuously as part of their indoctrination, but, whatever the cause, the result was that I was desperately lonely during my time there.

I had walked in the door of St Paul's as a naive country kid, excited to meet new people. When, after a couple of years of trying to make it work, I eventually moved into a flat by myself in Croydon, I was glad to get away from the snobbery of my college peers and into the wider world. Of course, with the passing of the years, people mellow, and I now consider some of those offenders to be good friends — although not too many of them are aligned with the Labor side of politics.

During my first three months at St Paul's College, I was to experience an event that I believe contributed to shaping my direction in life. As a teenager, like many other boys, I had developed a love of fast cars, and my father provided me with a Datsun 1600 from his car yard to drive to university. I assume that he and Mum thought I would be more likely to get back to see them in Forster regularly if I had a reliable car. Unfortunately, it was also a very fast and high-performing car for its class, and I knew what it was capable of, as Dad had driven me to school on numerous occasions in the same model.

In the first three months of 1970, I drove to Forster each weekend from Sydney to see my family and my friend Beth. In those days, it was a much longer trip on long and often winding single-lane roads. One Sunday night after one of these visits, I picked up a new-found friend, Peter Riddell, who was also living in St Paul's College, to return to Sydney. Just before we headed off, Peter's father, Gordon, stuck his head in the window for some friendly farewell banter.

'Looks like your seatbelt's coming loose,' he told Peter. 'The bolt's about to fall out. We need to fix that.'

I was annoyed, as I just wanted to get on the road for the seven-hour drive back to Sydney. 'It's been like that for a while,' I said. 'I think it's okay.'

Thankfully, Peter's dad wouldn't take no for an answer. 'I'm going to get a spanner. It'll only take a moment.'

We finally set off ten minutes later, and picked up another friend, Kaye Fitness. We dropped her off at Lochinvar, near Newcastle, which was lucky for her. Less than an hour later, going over 140 kilometres per hour, we took a corner, and I misjudged the angle and speed of the car. The Datsun flipped and rolled, and then continued to roll, overturning five or more times. We could hear the deafening crunch of metal on asphalt, and saw sparks and flashes of light flying around us, until finally, after about 40 seconds, the car came to a stop in the silence of the Australian bush. The Datsun was upside down, and had gone over the edge of a bridge. Peter and I were still in our seats, hanging upside down in creek bed, held in by only our seatbelts. We scrambled to release ourselves and get out of the upturned car. Both of us were extremely lucky to have survived. In an instant, we had been transformed from two bulletproof, invincible, testosterone-driven teenagers in a high-powered car into a pair of vulnerable prisoners, trapped in an uncontrollable, flimsy tin can, as it catapulted along until its energy, and nearly our lives, were exhausted. And there is no doubt that Peter would not have survived but for his father fixing his seatbelt before we set off from Forster.

The car was written off, and I was still getting glass out of my hair days later. I also had to suffer the ignominy of phoning my parents 150 kilometres away, waking them from their Sunday-night slumber to ask them to collect their reckless and irresponsible son from the Kurri Kurri Police Station. The accident was a huge wake-up call for me, and the near-death experience made me think hard about what was important in life. I understood that not only had I just barely cheated death, but I had also nearly killed a friend in the process. I realised that life was fragile, and I didn't want my life to be about striving for wealth and material possessions. What I really cared about was the love of people, including, of course, my family and friends. The accident was the catalyst for my becoming a much more compassionate person.

My growing awareness that I'd been living in a selfish, materialistic way was compounded by an event three days later, when I returned to St Paul's College to resume my studies. I had never been a church-goer, but I was still fragile and deeply reflective about what had just happened, and so I decided to take some time out in the small college chapel. I had always loved the design of this chapel, with its walls behind the altar emblazoned with hundreds of multi-coloured glass stones. They came to life when the sun shone on them, as it did that day in my moment of solitude.

I sat there for a long time, quietly thinking about our close escape. Absentmindedly — and most uncharacteristically — I picked up a Bible, which had been left on the pew in front of me. I randomly flipped it open, and my eyes fell

34

on these words: 'It is easier for a camel to pass through the eye of a needle than for a rich man to enter the kingdom of heaven.' I couldn't believe what I was reading. To me, it was a validation of my renunciation of the mindless pursuit of material possessions, which had occupied my thinking since the crash. I didn't see this moment as a religious experience or revelation, but for a very shaken up 18-year-old, it was a coincidence that affirmed the direction I wanted to take in life. To focus on doing what I could, in my own modest way, to contribute to building a better world.

As an aside, I want to note that I have only had one other substantial car accident in my life. The second took place only six months after the first, when I crashed into a taxi on Elizabeth Street in Sydney, as I was about to turn into Hunter Street. Peter Riddell was in the car with me then, too, and I accused him of being a jinx. He insisted it was me, and I admit that the weight of evidence was on his side.

4

Moving into politics

Outside college, my life was dominated by a demanding and highly competitive law course. I had embarked on a straight four-year law degree, skipping a preliminary arts degree, because, at the time, I wanted to go back to the country to live — I couldn't see my future in the city. I made some good friends at law school, including my best friend, Wendy Steed. I ended up being an articled clerk to Wendy's father, and became close friends with her mother, Rita. Tragically, Wendy was killed in a car accident when she was 26. I continued to visit her mother every Christmas for decades.

I'd become interested in politics before I left home for university, although my views had marked a sharp divide from the political views of my father, who was a member of the then-named Country Party, which would later become the National Party. After many years as a member, Dad resigned because it was too left-wing for him! I think his basic philosophy was that he'd had to struggle in life for his achievements, and he thought others should, too. It was a kind of survival-of-the-fittest approach to life in some ways, although my father was, in his heart, a kind and good person. My mother did not have any overt political views, but she always gave me the impression that she also voted for the National Party. She was, however, a deeply empathetic person who hated to see people hurting, and she had some sensitivity towards the Aboriginal population of the town.

I attended my first political demonstration in July 1971, right out the front of the Sydney Town Hall. It was a protest against the visiting South African Springbok Rugby team . My own political views were starting to take shape. I must have been still under my father's influence to a certain extent, however, because I also joined the Sydney University Liberal Club. It was connected to, but not part of, the Liberal Party, of which I was never a member. I was still very politically immature at that time, with unformed values, but joining this club was a tentative step towards exploring political parties. Through the club, I had the opportunity to meet Don Chipp, Andrew Peacock, and other senior Liberals of the time, although certainly none of them would have ever remembered me from those days.

It was as a fledgling University Liberal Club member that I went one day in early 1972, in the lead-up to the federal election of that year, to hear McMahon government minister Malcolm Fraser speak at the Ash Street headquarters of the New South Wales Liberal Party. That night, Mr Fraser was surrounded by doting Liberal Party followers, all rapturously applauding as he championed the school-funding rights of the very wealthiest non-government schools. I was instantly reminded of many of the residents of St Paul's College. I guess Mr Fraser was shaping his speech for his audience, but I was more interested in what he was going to do to fund the most disadvantaged schools in Australia, including country schools, and he said nothing of that. I realised I was in the wrong place. Within a short time of hearing Mr Fraser's speech, I had joined the Australian Labor Party (ALP).

I think that even his strongest supporters would agree that Malcolm Fraser mellowed hugely in his later life. By the time of his death, I held him in the highest regard, and we shared many common values, including the support for a more independent foreign policy for Australia and an abhorrence of racism. In my role as CEO of Australian Red Cross in 2005, I had the great privilege of meeting Malcolm Fraser again. I told him the story of my first encounter with him, and we shared a laugh. A couple of years later, I was extremely fortunate to work alongside his daughter Phoebe, when she headed up international humanitarian law at Red Cross.

I joined the ALP in Croydon, where I was then living, and, as a 21-year-old, I voted ALP for my ever first vote. It was the 1972 federal election — the election that brought Gough Whitlam's government to power. My joining the ALP, voting for Whitlam, and becoming politically active for progressive causes mortified my father, who'd had visions of me becoming the federal member for Lyne in the strong Country Party area where I grew up.

During these years, my cousin Robert Brown played a part in shaping my future direction in life. Robert was the son of my mum's sister Gladys, who had passed away in the 1950s. My parents had provided strong support to Robert when he was young and living with his brother John and their widowed father in Granville, and he had often visited us in Forster. Robert was a gentle, soft-spoken soul. He was a bohemian sculptor, working out of a studio in Palmer Street in Sydney's Woolloomooloo. His work was similar in style to the famous Robert Klippel's, who I think Robert studied with at one time. They both used scrap metal in many of their works. Where I had grown up on a diet of chops and veggies, Robert was a vegan. He was always nattily dressed, charming, and beautifully spoken, with a strong intellectual curiosity and the most wonderful incisive sense of humour. He lived in Forbes Street, around the corner from his studio, with the celebrated weaver Mona Hessing.

When I moved to Sydney, Robert became a special person in my life, and introduced me to a side of the city I never knew existed, taking me around in his old VW Kombi. The first time I visited his studio in Woolloomooloo, I was still living at college. I left the privileged and cloistered walls of St Paul's one Sunday and entered a house that was an almost completely burnt-out shell. Robert's crazy metal sculptures — made from industrial piping, old machine parts, and junk — filled the whole ground floor and extended into the open garden at the back. The rear wall of the house had been completely demolished, leaving the place exposed to the garden and the elements. The only liveable room was accessed by a rickety open staircase with grass matting on each stair. In the room was a double bed raised on a wooden platform.

The toilet was in the stairwell and was flushed with a bucket. Cockroaches seemed to be overrunning the place. The contrast with the college and my own conservative background could not have been more stark. And yet, I immediately felt at home in Woolloomooloo. So much so that in 1973 I moved from my place in Croydon and took up residence in Robert's studio. There, I instantly became an active member of the local ALP and the Woolloomooloo Resident Action Group.

Robert mixed with an amazing group of inner-city artists and political figures, including the cartoonist Bruce Petty, who had worked on one of his mechanical sculptures in Robert's studio in Palmer Street. The sculpture represented the complex working of the economy. With all its interlocking dependencies, it reminded me of my father's invented pool-cleaning device. Robert and his partner, Mona, also knew Germaine Greer from their circle of friends in the arts community. At their suggestion, I read her book *The Female Eunuch*. I was inspired by the book, but my naivety got me into trouble when I heard she was speaking at the Sydney University campus and I went to see her. After her talk, I went up and introduced myself as a friend of Robert and Mona, blurting out, 'I really admire your mind,' which was something only a country kid would do. She gave me a not-so-thinly-veiled look of utter contempt, put her hand on her hip, and said dismissively, 'And what do you think of my body?' I was mortified. I nervously muttered something incomprehensible and scurried away.

Even so, in less than four years, I had come a long way from my sheltered upbringing in Forster, and I was so happy living in Woolloomooloo. Every weekday morning I walked up past the Art Gallery of New South Wales, across the parkland of The Domain and towards the city's skyscrapers and the Sydney University Law School on the corner of King and Elizabeth Streets — a quintessentially Sydney start to the day.

Later, I rented a very run-down house at 83 Bourke Street, around the corner from Robert and Mona. A network of friends from Forster moved in, and then their friends moved in, and soon we spread into the house next door. We formed a little community of country kids in those dilapidated houses. One winter's night, we burnt the side fence separating the properties, and then we grew a bountiful garden joining the two houses. My friend Tim Gray played the guitar, and the house resonated with the songs of Leonard Cohen and Neil Young, and other music of the early seventies. We formed deep bonds; the friendships from those houses have lasted all my life. One of those bonds was with Christine Logan, who lived next door with her boyfriend of the time, and whom I would later marry. Diane Hudson became another close friend, who subsequently became my executive assistant and office manager when I was appointed minister.

My Woolloomooloo days were important to my personal development in other ways, too. Growing up an only child without a lot of physical contact with my father as I grew older had given me a limited concept of masculinity. There had been no sisters and brothers to fight with, or to hug and make peace with. Until these share houses, I'd never lived with anyone except my mum and dad. I was also quite shy with girls as a young man, and not a very tactile person with friends, especially male friends. This all changed when I moved into 83 Bourke Street. It was there that I learnt how to hug, and how to open up and give more of myself to others.

I also formed exceptionally strong friendships with some of the long-term residents of the area: waterside workers, builders, labourers, and trade-union activists. They welcomed me into their lives and supported and nurtured my political development, both inside and outside the ALP. We mixed together in local pubs, at ALP meetings, and at meetings of the Woolloomooloo Resident Action Group. We also worked together in support of the green bans implemented by the New South Wales branch of the Builders Labourers Federation to save the historic residential areas of the city of Sydney from redevelopment. The green bans were an industrial tactic by the union that empowered building workers to have a say about the consequences of their labour and gave them their right to refuse to demolish the historic buildings of Sydney — demolitions which were driving out low-income earners from the city. Both the green bans and the workers fighting for them were vilified at the time, especially in the tabloid media and on talkback radio, but now most informed people believe they saved the city. The union also stood up for housing for low-income earners, for Aboriginal rights, for the rights of same-sex couples, and against discrimination of all kinds at a time when discrimination was perfectly legal in this country.

Around this time, I also became a volunteer at the Wayside Chapel, serving some of the most marginalised members of the local community. There, I became friends with the late Ted Noffs, who had founded this wonderful Sydney institution, and I also met Bill Crews, who later continued his commitment to people by leading the Exodus Foundation in Ashfield in the inner west of Sydney. Working at the Wayside Chapel was a real privilege and introduced me to a very different world to the one I'd grown up in. I learnt so much about the challenges facing people who hadn't had the opportunities I'd had — people who were struggling to survive on the streets of Kings Cross, sometimes living in very poor circumstances, and sometimes struggling with mental illness or the impact of racism on their lives.

From the start, Mum and Dad were horrified that I'd moved to Woolloomooloo. They still saw it as a place of gangsters and razor gangs, which it had been known for before World War II. I had to work hard to give them confidence that things had changed and that I was safe there — which wasn't helped by the heroin addict next door, who regularly injected himself in front of the window facing our kitchen, or the proximity of the brothel that backed onto our house. Over that back fence, I had observed that the dogs that guarded the brothel were fed from time to time by a prominent member of the local ALP branch. I was always intrigued by the motivation behind those little acts of animal kindness, which demonstrated a closer relationship between politics and the underworld establishment than I cared to imagine.

The razor gangs had long gone, but Woolloomooloo was still a volatile and sometimes dangerous area. As a member of the Resident Action Group, I worked with Juanita Nielsen, an heiress of the wealthy Mark Foy's department-store family. She seemed to me to be a strong and well-intentioned advocate for good planning in the city, and she was always well briefed on the machinations of the city development industry. She was campaigning against the redevelopment of the historic houses of Victoria Street, Kings Cross, where she lived. I worked closely with her at various times: I visited her house for campaign meetings, and she once visited my grungy little share house in Woolloomooloo.

It is commonly known that Juanita Nielsen was murdered by those acting to thwart her campaign against the over-development of Victoria Street, though her body has never been recovered. Knowing her well, as I did, I was shocked and outraged by her disappearance and apparent murder. We had lost a dedicated, high-profile crusader for the public good. Juanita Nielsen's death was a chilling reminder of how high the stakes were in opposing the interests and plans of some big Sydney property developers at the time. Corrupt conduct by public officials and in the corporate sector in dealings with government has always sickened me. Throughout my life, I have always championed political reforms like ICAC, including at the national level, as they flush out, and hold people accountable for, corrupt conduct.

5

Sydney City Council

For me, the whole experience of those years in Woolloomooloo was transformative and opened up a completely new world of left-of-centre, community, and Labor politics. I became more determined than ever that I wanted to commit my life to the struggle for a more just and peaceful world.

At age 22, I came upon what may have been another fork in the road of my life. I had been very interested in acting at school, and, while living in Woolloomooloo, I had joined an amateur theatre group led by the well-respected actor Allan Penney. The group operated in an old church hall at 228 Forbes Street, Darlinghurst. I had been cast in a play that was to be performed in Newcastle, but to accept the part I was obliged to shave off the bushy beard I'd acquired. Meanwhile, I'd been preselected to stand as an ALP candidate for the Fitzroy ward in the 1974 Sydney City Council elections — an opportunity that had arisen when the previously chosen candidate had stood down at the last moment. This was my first chance to serve my community through elected public office. Crucially, the candidate photographs had been taken and the election material had been printed with a bearded me — shaving my beard off now was not an option if I wanted to go through with the election. I chose politics, declined the acting role, and the rest, as they say, is history.

I wasn't elected to the council in the 1974 election, but was, by then, a very dedicated environmentalist, partly in response to the rampant development of the city and partly to the sand mining occurring near Forster.

Although I was living in Sydney, I still had a deep love for the bush and especially for the north coast of New South Wales where I'd grown up. I established the Forster-Tuncurry Area Conservation Society, with me as president and my old friend Terry taking on the role of secretary. We campaigned on local issues for a few years, but I was travelling to Forster for various public meetings of the group, and eventually the tyranny of distance made it impossible for me to continue.

Back in Sydney, I was passionately committed to a very different future for the city than that advocated by the aldermen and the political party who controlled the council. The party in power was called the Civic Reform Association, and it was dominated by the interests of property developers in the city. The Civic Reform Association wasn't the Liberal Party operating in the local government arena of the Sydney City Council, although it enjoyed their support. Rather, it was a separately incorporated entity, with major corporate vested interest groups as part of its formal structure, including the Master Builders Association. These groups, and their members, were profiting from the demolition of the historic buildings of the city and the rapacious pursuit of development at all costs. I was particularly outraged by the destruction of heritage buildings and the threat to whole neighbourhoods — Woolloomooloo was at risk, and so were many other communities.

Low-income earners and the long-term working-class residents of the city were being forced out by bad planning decisions. I wanted to be elected to the council and had a real conviction that this was my calling. I moved to Surry Hills and began to develop a political platform to drive deep changes in Sydney City government, which for a hundred years had been dominated either by big business interests or by the right wing of the ALP. I was strongly supported by two wonderful working-class mentors, Fred Miller and Len Devine, who welcomed me into their Surry Hills homes. They believed in me and actively supported my aspirations in the ALP. Len was the former federal MP for East Sydney, and Fred later became the state member for Bligh. I am forever grateful for their kindness and that of their families. At the time, I had ambitions to be the federal member for Sydney, but, as fate would have it, this was not to be. My opportunity to serve in the national parliament did arise later, although by another and somewhat unexpected pathway.

In 1974, I also began teaching law at the New South Wales Institute of Technology. Later in the year, I worked as the manager of the New South Wales Environment Centre, which was located on Broadway near the intersection with Glebe Point Road. I was in this office when I heard the news of the dismissal of the Whitlam government on 11 November 1975, and, with thousands of other people, joined the big spontaneous protest march in the city streets that afternoon.

Some months later, in August 1976, I organised a creative demonstration against Governor-General Sir John Kerr at Sydney's Wentworth Hotel in response to Kerr's unconstitutional dismissal of the Whitlam government and the appointment of Malcolm Fraser as prime minister. It involved a dignified but highly effective walk-out of a Sydney University Law Graduates' Association luncheon, where the guest speakers were Sir John Kerr, Chief Justice of the High Court Sir Garfield Barwick, and Bob Ellicott QC, who was the Fraser government's attorney-general at the time. All three men had been participants in the events surrounding and following the dismissal of the Whitlam government. Network TV cameras filmed the walk-out, and all major papers covered the story. The special branch of the New South Wales police force stood by impassively as we conducted our peaceful objection. Many of my fellow protesters went on to become prominent lawyers, judges, and state government ministers.

There was an over-the-top *Sydney Morning Herald* editorial on 4 August 1976 condemning our actions. The editorial asserted that 'there is a danger that in emphasising the puerility of individual "protests" of this kind the reality of what we are witnessing in the campaign against the Governor General is obscured. It should not be. The campaign is a sinister one, mounted, co-ordinated and paid for by sinister people for sinister reasons. The purpose of the campaign is to create a climate of violence, intimidation and harassment.' Such a ridiculously extreme response was utterly unwarranted: we had engaged in expressing our right of freedom of speech in a peaceful protest about an issue of deep concern to almost 50 per cent of the Australian people. This extreme editorial was the inspiration the very next day for Frank Hardy and Donald Horne to decide to form 'Citizens for Democracy', a national protest movement that organised huge rallies around Australia in support of constitutional reform and in opposition to the sacking of an elected government by the governor-general. I became part of the organising committee.

During 1976, I moved out of Woolloomooloo and rented a house at 423 Crown Street, Surry Hills — just a few blocks from the hospital where I was born. I lived in a tiny attic at the top of the house for two years, paying for the environment group Friends of the Earth to operate in the two floors below, and participating in their work and activities. I also established a free local newspaper called *The People's Paper*, funded by my own modest income and by advertising. Through this, I championed progressive environmental and social policies, and attacked what I saw as corruption in the Sydney City Council.

It was also around this time that I did something that my parents thankfully never found out about; as committed golfers, they would have been horrified by my actions. I was a vehement opponent of the South African apartheid regime, and so I attended a demonstration against visiting South African golfer Gary Player. I didn't set out to get charged, but my determination to stand by my convictions led to me being arrested and moved off the golf course by Inspector Longbottom, who was the head of the special branch of the New South Wales police. This moment was captured in a much-publicised photograph of me, Inspector Longbottom, and fellow-protester Meredith Burgmann, who later became the president of the New South Wales Legislative Council. I was taken to the local police station, fingerprinted, and charged with a public-order offence, which I recall was 'disturbing the peace'. I was subsequently acquitted of the charge in court.

In 1977, I was elected to the Sydney City Council as an alderman representing the Flinders ward, which included Surry Hills, Centennial Park, and South Paddington. The council became much of my life for the next six years, and, together with my progressive colleagues Steve McGoldrick, Tony Reeves, and later Stan Ashmore-Smith, we championed many social and political issues in one of the most controversial and reforming periods in council history. During that time, the Civic Reform lord mayor and a major Sydney corporation were exposed in the media as having engaged in improper conduct, long before there was any ICAC. Tony Reeves led the exposure of their secret dealings, which ended up on the front page of the *National Times* newspaper and in a tabloid called *The Sunday*. The lord mayor tragically died on the day the material was published.

Through our council work, we were able to help shape a transformation in the policies of the city on environmental issues, town planning, and community services to better serve the residential areas and to support the greening of the central business district. A lot of things we did were in parallel with some of the more popular and mainstream policies of the progressive Greater London Council, such as our strong stand in opposition to racism and our stand on nuclear issues, but we certainly weren't emulating their model and had our own plans for Sydney. I am proud of the fact that many of the issues we stood up for all those years ago have since gained support in the community: energy conservation, urban forests, renewable energy, regional cycle ways, greening city buildings, rooftop gardens, and many more. Even so, some other issues we strongly supported still haven't been embraced by New South Wales governments of any political persuasion. In particular, wider metropolitan Sydney still lacks an effective public transport strategy.

One policy our council implemented was to level a 2 per cent tax on new development in the city centre to fund low-income housing. We didn't want Sydney to be a city just for the rich; we wanted it to be a place that supported a social mix of people. But not everyone agreed — most notably the state Labor government of Neville Wran. It was this policy that, I believe, prompted the state government to take radical action to regain control of our council. In 1981, they amalgamated the Sydney City Council with the perceived Labor Right-controlled South Sydney Council to create a mega-council with 27 elected aldermen. The legislation to do this was introduced without notice by the state government on the night of the press gallery Christmas party. The incoming city councillors stripped the progressive aldermen of their positions, even removing our desks and dumping papers and possessions into cardboard boxes. My colleagues took their cardboard boxes and held a media conference on the front steps of the Town Hall. Happily, the alliance which took over the council soon fell apart, and my colleagues and I were reinstated to our leadership positions.

Despite our political differences, my mum and dad were proud that I'd been elected to the council in 1977 — and re-elected in 1980. My father still would have preferred me not to be an ALP councillor, and he wrote me a letter at one stage suggesting that I should form a political party of my own. When I visited Forster, we would get into angry political debates. I would fly to Taree and be met by Mum and Dad, and before we got out of the airport, Dad and I would be fiercely raging against each other's political views. My mother tried to keep the peace as best she could, but we were both of strong convictions, and as a young man I was hot-headed and unforgiving. It sure made dinner conversation volatile and unpredictable.

My father remained a lifelong advocate of the conservative side of politics until he passed away, but I still loved him very much as my dad. Mum, on the other hand, gave out ALP how-to-vote cards for me in the city-council elections, much to my father's disdain. She even handed one to Patrick White at the Centennial Park booth, and I'm sure I got his vote. When I was acting lord mayor for a brief time in 1983, I honoured my mother by making her the acting lady mayoress when I hosted a scheduled civic reception on behalf of the city for a visiting delegation.

During this time, I was a high-profile figure in Sydney and appeared regularly in the media, championing a wide range of political causes as a city alderman. I was often in *The Sydney Morning Herald* and News Limited papers and on the nightly TV news, as well as speaking on radio, which was my favourite medium. The Sydney City Council never seemed to be out of the news in those days. For the first time in my life, I secretly wondered if my birth parents ever saw me and perhaps recognised a family resemblance.

My dad, though it pains me to say it, had very prejudiced views towards Aboriginal people — views that were deeply ingrained and a product of growing up in a different era. Working on tackling and changing this ugly underbelly of prejudice in Australian society was to become a large part of my life's work both inside and outside the Parliament of Australia, but I'm sure my father must have been mortified when, in 1978, his son left his secure and tenured job as a law lecturer to become a lawyer working for the Aboriginal Legal Service (ALS). I stayed there for the next six years, until I was elected to the House of Representatives in March 1984.

The ALS was based in Redfern and covered much of New South Wales, from the Queensland border to the Murray River, and out into the central west of the state. The solicitors and Aboriginal field officers were wonderful people to work with, and we formed bonds of friendship that have lasted throughout the years. In six years, I learnt so much about the way Aboriginal people have been treated in this country.

One of the many high-profile cases I was involved in concerned the shooting of a young Aboriginal man, Ronald 'Cheeky' McIntosh, in the town of Moree in 1982. He was shot dead by some non-Aboriginal men, and two others were wounded in the attack. The town became a powder keg, with the local Aboriginal community both enraged and grieving for their loss. My boss at ALS, a young Paul Coe, judged that we urgently needed to send legal reinforcements to Moree and asked me and another solicitor, Chris Lawrence, to book a flight and 'get up there immediately'. All the flights were booked out, but we could get one two days later. Paul hit the roof and told us angrily, 'Charter a plane and get up there now!' I couldn't believe what he was saying. Budgets were tight, and the ALS didn't charter planes; that was something only rich people did. But Paul insisted, and he was right to do so — once we got up there, we found the town in crisis.

We arrived at the Moree ALS office to find a huge meeting of local Aboriginal people being addressed by the police minister, Peter Anderson, and one of the deputy commissioners of police. The room was packed, with standing room only, and everyone was openly weeping, the minister and deputy police commissioner included. Most of the Aboriginal people were distraught and many were wailing uncontrollably. I will never forget the sight as long as I live, it was just so sad and distressing.

Chris and I worked with our local colleagues to get on top of the issues and talked to as many people as we could to give support to the community. We then took a few minutes out to have a coffee at a local milk bar and fell into conversation with the proprietor, at which point the most amazing thing happened.

'What you fellas doing in town?' he asked.

We told him we worked for the ALS and were here for the next few days, at least — until things settled down.

'It's a scary place right now, and we don't know what's going to happen next,' he said. 'Funny you blokes are in here, because earlier today my girl [his staff member] stopped work to talk to her boyfriend who came in to see her. They were talking about the killing, then she got upset and ran off, and I haven't seen her since.'

We knew immediately that we had found one of the perpetrators. We went straight to the Sydney Homicide Squad team leader and reported what we'd heard. Not long after, the offenders were apprehended and subsequently convicted of manslaughter.

I learnt a big life lesson through that experience, when reflecting on Paul Coe's response. As a leader, when you're confronted with a critical situation, you need to stay cool, be prepared to make big, courageous calls, and back your decision.

6

Losing my father

By 1983, I'd had enough of council politics and decided to take a new direction in my life. Serving as an elected member of the Sydney City Council had been a privilege, allowing me to become deeply involved in all aspects of city governance and planning — issues that remain close to my heart to this day. But the amalgamation of the South Sydney Council with the Sydney City Council had resulted in a council with members bitterly divided across party and factional lines. The impact of all this was demoralising. I had done my best, but it was time to move on.

I moved from Redfern, where I was then living, to rent a tiny house in Stanwell Park, a beautiful little seaside town in North Wollongong. I purchased a piano and started taking lessons, and bought myself another surfboard. But a balanced and normal life was not to be. As fate would have it, I had moved to the right place at the right time, and, in 1984, I stood for preselection for the federal seat of Hughes. The retiring member, Les Johnson, had left unexpectedly to take up an appointment as high commissioner to New Zealand. Despite appearances, this wasn't some grand plan on my part, but when this opportunity suddenly presented itself, I found that my lifelong commitment to politics drove me forwards, and I decided to go for it.

I won preselection against the opposition of the New South Wales Right of the ALP, and without the formal support of some prominent figures on the left of the party. I was able to prevail despite the strong campaign waged by the longstanding and respected president of the ALP Federal Electorate Council, Professor Jim Hagan, who had written a history of the ACTU and was supported by Bob Hawke. I was lucky to receive the preferences of a highly respected female candidate, Hazel Wilson. But what I also had was the support of a very strong majority of the local people after preferences were distributed, and to them I owe so much for the opportunity that was given to me.

I had one final hurdle to cross. The year before my election, I'd been arrested for allegedly pulling down the New South Wales Parliament House fence during an Aboriginal Land Rights demonstration. That sounds a rather herculean feat, but I was one person in a larger peaceful political protest of about 20 or 30 protesters. We had been demonstrating against the passage of legislation that retrospectively validated the past illegal revocation of Aboriginal Reserves, and also against the fact that Aboriginal people were denied access to the building while the Aboriginal Land Rights Act was being debated inside. We were standing on the stone foundation of the approximately two-metre-high wrought-iron fence at the front of the parliament, shaking it. Unfortunately, the fence gave way directly in the spot where I was standing, and I was charged with malicious damage. No one else had been charged, just me, even though it beggared belief that I could have been the sole person responsible for the suddenly sagging fence. I was placed in a nearby paddy wagon, and, through the metal grill on the door, I could see a very angry Charlie Perkins outside wanting to help me. In the end, there was nothing we could do. Some of my critics would later cheekily accuse me of 'doing anything to get into parliament'.

The demonstration had continued, but I was taken away in the paddy wagon. I was taken to Central Police Station, charged, fingerprinted, and released. I'd thought that this time I should let my mum and dad know about my day, so I phoned them in Forster from a phone box in the city. They were initially shocked and dismayed, but by the end of call were glad to know that I was okay, and that I had stood up for my beliefs.

By the time the case got to court, I had just been elected as a federal member of parliament. If they convicted me, I would be in danger of disqualification under section 44 of the Australian Constitution, which disqualified a member who was 'under sentence or subject to be sentenced' for an offence with a sentence greater than 12 months. I was humbled to receive references from a wide range of people in my life, including my old sparring partner on the Sydney City Council, Jeremy Bingham, and the Reverend Ted Noffs. Ultimately, no conviction was recorded and my legal advisors confirmed that the constitution was not breached and I could continue my parliamentary career. I became a very active backbench member of parliament, immersing myself in humanitarian and human-rights issues, while also demonstrating a wide policy interest across the work of government. Importantly, I also focused on being a dedicated local member, and, because of my history and country background, sought to engage with all local communities.

I felt particularly privileged to have the opportunity to serve in the Old Parliament House, so steeped in the history of our country as it is. Most nights, I used to work into the early hours of the morning in my Parliament House office, and, every night, even in the Canberra winter, I would ride my pushbike the 6 km to the suburb of O'Connor, where I rented a room and lived very simply. I have one special memory from these late nights, before the advent of security cameras and the like, when, after everyone else had left the building, I followed a cheeky impulse and gently pedalled my bike across grand, empty King's Hall on my way out.

One person who hugely influenced me during my political years was Tom Uren, whom I later became connected to through marriage, though in a different way to the ways most people become family through marriage. When I was 25, I had married my friend Christine Logan. Christine had also grown up in Forster, attending the same high schools as me, but a few years behind. We became an item after living next door to one another in Woolloomooloo, and that relationship translated into a relatively young marriage. I think we mainly got married because we were very happy and wanted to have a party and celebrate with our family and friends. Within a week of getting married, I was in a preselection ballot for the forthcoming 1977 Sydney City Council elections; two years later, my life had gone completely down the political path. Christine's life took a different path: she became deeply engaged with theatre and opera, eventually ending up in the chorus of the Australian Opera. Once we decided to divorce, our relationship almost immediately morphed back into friendship, and we have remained friends ever since. When Christine told me a couple of years later that she had fallen in love with Tom Uren, I was so happy for them both, as I already felt great love and admiration for this man who had so much warmth and integrity. Tom and Christine had 30 years together until he passed away on Australia Day in 2015.

Tom became an even greater influence on my life after I was elected as the federal member for Hughes, and, during his last years as a parliamentarian, we ended up with offices opposite each other in the new Parliament House — Tom with a very young Anthony Albanese staffing his office. I felt so close to Tom, and we shared many common values. He taught me how to love people more openly and warmly and how to give more of myself to others. Over time, I also noticed we shared the common feature of a large bottom jaw. Sometimes, my mind would play tricks on me, and I wondered if we could be related in some way. It was another of those rare times in my early years when my mind turned to my adoption and the fact that I didn't know my heritage.

Dad, despite his own personal political views, was proud to see me sworn in as the federal member for Hughes in 1984. Our relationship had changed significantly since 1977, when Dad's local dentist had diagnosed him with cancer of the mouth, and my father underwent a serious operation during which part of his tongue and neck were removed. Dad had had to learn to talk again with this impediment.

There was no doubt in my mind that Dad's cancer was a result of the tens of thousands of cigarettes that had been hanging out of the corner of his mouth for many decades. When he was diagnosed, I became an anti-tobacco warrior from that day forward. As a Sydney City Council member, I initiated a ban on tobacco advertising on council properties. When I became a federal member of parliament, I was one of the leaders of the campaign to successfully ban smokeless tobacco (chewing tobacco) in Australia. Later in parliament, I also introduced a private member's Bill to ban tobacco advertising in the Australian Capital Territory. This Bill didn't proceed to a vote, but it helped turn up the temperature on the tobacco industry. To this day, I remain a dedicated opponent of that industry and find it particularly insidious that it actively promotes its product in developing countries as its markets in other economies dry up.

Until his operation, Dad had never been in a hospital in his life, and he was terrified of them — even though he was the kind of stoic person of his generation who never complained. Mum and I were by his bedside in Royal Prince Alfred Hospital in Sydney after the operation, and it was a shock to hear him groaning in pain and see him so deeply distressed about his situation. As he was unable to talk properly, the doctors had encouraged him to write notes to communicate. He wrote a note and passed it to me, and I saw that this tough, resilient, and courageous man had written 'I wish I were dead'.

I quickly hid the note from my mother and diverted her attention to other things, but she was too smart for me. Later, outside Dad's room, she asked me what he'd written.

'Nothing,' I said. 'It was just a scrawl.'

'Show me, please. Right now,' she demanded.

I passed her the note. We fell into each other's arms and comforted each other until, a long time later, the tears stopped flowing.

When we returned to the ward, I blurted out, 'We love you, Dad, and you're going to be okay,' and put my head gently on his side, trying not to cry again. It was about as close as I could get to him, because every other part of his body seemed to have a high-tech medical device or tube coming out of it.

After that, things were never the same again. Dad and I were suddenly free to show our love for each other, verbally and physically. I could hug and kiss him on the cheek with open warmth and affection. He was freer with his displays of affection to my mother as well. So when the cancer returned as a brain tumour in 1985, my ability to show my dad effusive warmth and love knew no bounds. Together, my mother and I showed him our immense love and support.

I recall one hilarious experience when Dad was in St Vincent's Hospital having radiation treatment after his brain tumour had taken away the use of his arms. They lay useless by his sides as he sat in the hospital chair waiting for a shave from the hospital support worker. My mother and I spotted the wardsman approaching with an old-fashioned razor blade in hand, and we saw that he was Aboriginal. I suddenly realised that Dad, with his old prejudices, might be seeing himself as the man from Ironbark, about to get his throat cut by the barber. Instead, to my delight, Dad's sense of humour was still strong, even though his brain had been affected by the tumour and the heavy drugs he was taking. He pointed to the wardsman and said to Mum and me, 'Rob's mate, Rob's mate,' then gave his new-found friend a warm and welcoming smile. My mother and I completely cracked up. Dad had finally got it: we're all part of the human family. I'm delighted to report that the shave proceeded with no loss of blood and with all four of us laughing together.

I think that most of us remember, or will remember, the circumstances of the death of our parents, and I remember the passing of my father with vivid clarity. It happened in June 1985, at a time when political commitments had taken me away from him — something that still causes me pain now. Dad had finished his radiation treatment in Sydney and was flown back to Forster hospital in poor shape, but expecting to live for some time. As a backbench MP, I was active in the campaign for an independent Timor-Leste, and was invited to go to Darwin to participate in a radio link-up with the Fretilin fighters, who were still in the country's mountains all these years after the Indonesian invasion in 1975. We went to a remote location in the bush where the radio link was successfully established, including with the Fretilin leader and future president Xanana Gusmão.

Afterwards, instead of flying back to Sydney and heading to Forster to be with Dad, I had to go straight to Canberra for an unusual one-day sitting of the House of Representatives.

I was in my office in the House of Representatives side of Old Parliament House when the bells rang for a division. During my years in parliament, I was respectful of and close to the attendants and support staff, and, on this day, when my mum called the main switchboard, they recognised the urgency of her call and tracked me down en route to the division.

Mum simply said, 'Rob, we've lost Dad. He passed away just now.'

At first, I didn't believe it. My father couldn't die when I wasn't there with him and with my mother. I hung on to the phone, hearing my mother's distressed state, wanting to give her comfort, and not wanting to let go. All the while, the bells for the division kept ringing loudly and relentlessly just above my head.

A mob of my ALP colleagues surged past, heading for the chamber for the vote. Unaware of my situation, they told me to drop the phone and get into the chamber or I'd miss the division — almost a hanging offence for a member of parliament. And still the bells kept ringing.

I had no choice but to tell Mum, 'Sorry, I've got to go,' and in a mix between a state of shock and a trance, I ran towards the chamber. I got there with just a second to spare. As the Speaker of the house called, 'Lock the doors,' the old glass doors of the House of Representatives slammed shut behind me.

I was in a daze and struggled to find my seat. Despite the chatter and commotion of the house, I was somehow weirdly sensitive to every sound in the chamber. I could hear the whip, Ben Humphries, a long way away, telling the ministers on the front bench, including Prime Minister Bob Hawke, 'Tickner's father just died.'

I'd already had strong disagreements with Bob on policy, even though I'd only been in the parliament as a humble backbench member for a very short time. So I was greatly touched when, after the division and the conclusion of the vote, he immediately came to the back of the chamber where I sat, stunned and distressed, between my colleagues Jeannette McHugh and Peter Baldwin, with tears streaming down my face. Bob hugged me, and I was deeply comforted by that small but genuinely caring gesture. It again reminded me of how important it is that people shouldn't be afraid to show emotion and affection, to reach out to comfort those who may need it. We should never be afraid to show our humanity.

When Dad died, Mum lost her soulmate and partner of 50 years. In 1991, she moved, with my support, out of the family home and into a more convenient and easier-to-manage unit in Tuncurry. She bravely soldiered on, but life would never be the same.

I was absolutely devoted to her, but I was a federal MP, working in what became a marginal seat as the result of a redistribution. Life was busy, and, from 1988, I had additional demanding responsibilities as the chair of the Joint Standing Committee of Public Accounts, as well as being very involved as the chair of the Amnesty International Parliamentary Group. I did my best, but I couldn't always be with her in Forster, much as I wanted to support and care for her.

In early 1990, following the election of that year, I was allocated the role of minister for Aboriginal and Torres Strait Islander affairs by Prime Minister Bob Hawke, and my life became even more consumed by a whirlwind of travel and responsibilities. These demands left me only able to spend one or two nights at home in Stanwell Park, and with very few opportunities to get to Forster-Tuncurry, although I was on the phone to Mum regularly to monitor her wellbeing.

Sadly, after Dad's death, my mum developed dementia, and it came hard and fast. I returned from a short trip to Tonga and phoned her as soon as I landed to check she was okay, as I always did. However, this time I found the phone disconnected. I quickly organised with Telstra for an immediate reconnection and was able to confirm that Mum was fine. I worked out that she'd forgotten to pay the account, which seemed very unlike her, so I immediately dropped everything, jumped in the car, and drove to Forster-Tuncurry to take stock of the situation. I am grateful that I caught things just on the cusp, as my mum was about to descend into a critical phase of decline. While I had noticed some different behaviour over that past year, I didn't appreciate the pace of the deterioration, and Mum had been cleverly giving me the impression that she was coping.

When I got to her unit in Tuncurry, I discovered the cheque for the Telstra account in her purse. She had forgotten to post it. I then found that there was virtually no food in the fridge, and the budgie I'd bought her for company was lying in its cage, apparently starved to death. It was a sad situation indeed, and I felt terrible that I could have been so blind to the signs of rapid deterioration caused by this wretched condition. I think my mother was just so proud, so heroic, that she'd continued to push on with her life while it was falling apart around her.

Through the wonderful Dr Sanders, I was able to secure immediate accommodation in a nearby aged-care accommodation complex called GLAICA, just around the corner from the unit in Tuncurry where Mum had been living. She had her own attractive self-contained room there, but moving her into it was one of the hardest experiences of my life.

At first, she refused to even consider leaving the unit. I stood with her in her small kitchen, pleading with her to move.

'Mum, please can you understand, it's just not safe for you living here on your own anymore. What if you left the stove on by accident?'

I marshalled every angle of persuasion at my disposal: 'Mum, it's what Dad would have wanted'; 'Doctor Sanders thinks it's the best thing to do.' But I failed miserably.

By now, Mum was crying, and my heart just melted. She looked so tiny and vulnerable standing there in her kitchen. But despite my best efforts at persuasion, she was still point-blank refusing to consider moving.

And so I broke down, too. Tears streamed down my cheeks as I despaired of what to do. How on earth was I going to convince her that it wasn't safe for her to continue to live alone? I'd already immobilised Dad's old car, which she'd still been driving just six months earlier, but now it was no longer possible to be confident of her walking to the local shops alone and finding her way home.

To my amazement, my waterfall of tears brought a new response from my wonderful, compassionate mother. 'Well, Rob, if it's upsetting you that much, I will do it.'

I was bowled over, and filled with relief and love for her. But the worst was yet to come.

I had the move organised like a well-oiled machine, or so I thought. I took Mum to the aged-care accommodation for a cup of tea as a first step, as advised. The staff told me that I had to get Mum to make the shift, and that whatever way I did it there would be a degree of trauma. I knew they were right, and that it was now or never. So while Mum drank her cup of tea and chatted to the staff, I jumped into the car, rushed back to the unit, and packed as many personal items as I could into some large cardboard boxes. I grabbed clothes, photographs of Dad and me, and ornaments and pictures to make the new room as homely and familiar as possible. I crammed the boxes into the car and rushed back to GLAICA. In a matter of half an hour, I had completely furnished Mum's new room.

It looked very welcoming, but after I'd got Mum settled and was preparing to leave, she began to cry.

'Rob, please don't leave me here,' she pleaded.

I thought I would die then and there on the spot. I'd prepared the room so well, but to no avail.

'But, Mum, we agreed you'd be safer and happier here,' I said, trying to reassure her.

But her tears kept flowing. 'Please don't leave me, Rob. I don't want to be here. Take me home — this isn't where I live.'

It was hard to argue against her logic, but I knew that allowing my mother to live on her own with rapidly on-setting dementia would be both cruel and irresponsible.

The nurses looking after my mother saw my raw anguish, but told me that there was only one way to do this: leave and come back the next day.

I don't know how I found the strength to leave my mother that day. I was so distressed I barely found my way to the car. Even now, over 27 years later, I don't know if I did the right thing. Like all of us who are confronted by this wretched condition in our beloved parents, the only possibility is to stumble on with the best advice available. I'm not proud of the fact, but I self-medicated that night with most of a bottle of Scotch and cried myself to sleep, riddled with desperation, guilt, and shame.

The next day, to my utter bewilderment, I found Mum relaxed and completely settled in her new home, with no hint of unease or unhappiness. The room looked great, the staff were attentive and caring, and, most importantly of all, my mother was happy. She was pleased to see me, and at the end of my visit she farewelled me with a reassuring wave at the front door. It was as if she had lived there for years.

Mum settled even more over time, and I continued to visit her regularly and keep in contact by phone every couple of days. I often took her out for a drive and to buy her favourite 'frothy coffee' by the water at the little village of Smiths Lake, near Forster. Through some strange twist of her mind, Mum never again mentioned the unit she'd left behind, even though she'd lived there for years. When she did occasionally speak of her longing for her home, it was for our family home, which she'd moved out of almost ten years earlier. I can only surmise that she'd been so desperately lonely in the unit without Dad that she suppressed all memory of it, from the day she left it to the day she passed away two years later.

7

Beautiful Baby Jack

In 1986, my life had changed again when I had married Joanne (Jody) Hutchings, who was the granddaughter of one of my mother's sisters, and therefore my first cousin once removed. Because I was adopted into the family, there was of course no genetic relationship between Jody and me. I had first seen her back in 1960, when I was staying at my grandmother's house in Merrylands as an eight-year-old boy. Jody was a tiny baby then, and her parents left her with my grandmother while they went out that night. I think it was the first time I had significant contact with a baby, and I found it intriguing and memorable. After Jody's parents divorced, her mother, Jenny, took her and her brother, Danny, to live in Forster, and later married a local Forster identity, Maurie Burton. I had left Forster by then, but met Jody again through her father, Don, my cousin, who provided personal comfort and support to me when my father died in 1985.

When Jody and I married, I became the instant and devoted father of her daughter, Jade, who was then six. That Jody, as a single mother, was able to keep Jade when she was born, and build such an amazingly close relationship with her, is a testimony not only to Jody's parenting skills, but also to the complete change in social attitudes since I was born in 1951.

Then on 28 September 1992, Jack Edward Tickner came into the world. To say his arrival changed my life is such an understatement; the day of his birth was one of the most remarkable I have ever experienced. I know it's a big call, but that day I got a huge insight into the meaning of life.

Jody's contractions began the night before at about 11.00 pm, and so all three of us bundled into the car for the 45-minute trip to Sutherland Hospital. Progress was brought to a screeching halt on the Princes Highway at Engadine when a huge huntsman spider appeared on the inside of the windscreen, just in front of Jody. Remedial action was undertaken, but it must have looked funny to passers-by seeing a heavily pregnant woman bolting from a car by the side of the highway.

We got to the hospital in plenty of time, and Jade and I took up residence in the waiting room until I was called into the birth in the early hours of the morning. It was another world to me, as I'd been unable to attend most of Jody's birthing classes due to the pressure of ministerial and electorate responsibilities — and when I had attended, my mind was usually elsewhere, as it frequently was during those years in public life. I did, however, take a strong interest in the baby's development; I even asked the gynaecologist to take a sound recording of the baby's heart in the womb, which I still have. He said he'd never been asked to do that in 40 years of medical practice, but it seemed like a good idea to me.

Not only had I flunked the birthing classes, but babies generally were a relatively foreign species to me. The closest I'd got to one in recent years was when a new mother, and one of my strong supporters, proudly introduced her baby to me at a community function and asked me to hold it for a while. I jokingly declined to kiss the baby for fear of being labelled a sleazy, vote-grabbing politician by the media who were present. I didn't have any family or close friends with babies, and of course there'd been no baby sisters or brothers in the house when I was growing up. Nevertheless, although I'd been a failure at birthing classes and knew next-to-nothing about babies, I tried to be a good support person at the birth. I'd had no prior conception of how incredibly hard giving birth was: I was full of admiration for Jody and the way she kept her cool.

When Jack was born, I was asked to cut the umbilical cord. Overcome with joy, I hammed it up, pretending we were at an official event, like the opening of a building or a new road. I took the scissors, said, 'I am honoured to be here as your local member of parliament, and I have great pleasure in now declaring Jack officially open,' and cut the cord. I still have a media clipping from *The Australian* the next day, reporting my impromptu speech.

Jody took Jack in her arms, and I gazed in awe at this little person we'd created. Later that day, holding Baby Jack myself, I remember being in an almost transcendental state, absolutely amazed by his existence, and so very privileged that this life-changing event had happened to me. It also came to me that this little person was the first human on the planet who I knew was biologically related to me. It was a very special feeling.

Like many adopted people, it was the birth of my child that drew me into new territory. Until now in my life, I had honestly discounted the significance of blood relationships; for me, my mother, father, aunties, uncles, and cousins were an integral part of my life. I never felt other than a very connected and engaged member of my family, which just happened to be an adopted family. But right from the beginning, there was something about this tiny baby in my arms that was different. I had helped create this little person, and I was deeply moved by the intensity of my feelings for him. I began to think about what looks and characteristics he may have inherited from me, which in turn took me gradually on an introspective journey to ponder my own genetic inheritance over time and the link that Jack would have to that inheritance. Indeed, I began to consider the meaning of my own life and my wider place in the greater human family. Jack's birth was therefore, in many ways, the catalyst for my change of heart and my increasing resolve that perhaps the time had come to lift the veil and see if my birth family were still alive — and, if so, whether they were remotely interested in meeting me.

I would not have taken this step if my mother Gwen had not by now slipped into a world of her own because of dementia. In fact, only two years earlier in 1990, when the adoption laws had changed in New South Wales and it became possible for an adopted person to search for his or her birth parents, I'd been quite hostile to the idea. I'd felt, as I had all my life, that my mum and dad were my parents, and that, while Mum was alive, I would never seek out my birth family. In my mind, that would have been an act of betrayal and potentially hurtful to Mum. Not that she ever did or said anything to make me think this would be the case, but I didn't want to do anything to risk causing her even the slightest pain. I owed her everything, and my loyalty to her was absolute. It was with all these feelings in mind that I'd stopped in at the Rockdale office of the Department of Community Services on 22 March 1991 and lodged a contact veto, which prevented my birth mother or anyone else contacting me, should they be alive or interested. I had no concept of the extent to which my birth mother could be still grieving deeply for the child she gave away all those years ago.

By the time of Jack's birth, I knew that nothing I did could cause my mother Gwen pain or discomfort. She was living in a comfortable and secure place and was well protected from any adverse consequences that might come of me moving forward. So, in the months ahead, I began to ask myself questions about my birth mother. Was she still alive? If she was, would she want to meet me? Would I look like her? Which of her qualities had I inherited? Would meeting her give me insights into myself and deepen my understanding of my own life?

My longing for this meeting became intense, and I knew the time had come. I had finally realised, after 41 years, that I wanted to know where I came from.

During the latter part of 1992, after Jack was born, I regularly used to drive past the Department of Community Services office — the same office where I'd lodged the contact veto — on my way to attend meetings in the city. Now my thoughts turned to getting the veto lifted. To be honest, in my heart of hearts, I was increasingly disappointed that no attempt had been made to contact me. Despite the veto, I would have been notified if there had been an attempt. Was there anyone out there? Or had I left it too late? Without properly thinking through a plan of action, I decided to take the first steps: lift the contact veto, then get my original birth certificate.

With a rare moment to spare one day, I called in to the Rockdale office. It provided a range of government services, and anything related to adoption would have been a very small part of their work. For a while, I stood at the counter having second thoughts about whether I was doing the right thing. I felt quite insecure and wanted to be very private about this, which would be difficult, as I had a high profile in Sydney at the time.

A woman came to the counter, and I took a deep breath and launched into my quest. 'Good afternoon. I'd like to speak to someone about proceeding with an adoption reunion process, please.'

The woman explained to me that the staff member who handled adoption issues wasn't available that day. My heart sank, and I was sure the entire office heard it hit the floor.

'Forgive me, but I have a very demanding job, and it's difficult for me to get to the office. Is there anyone else who could help me?' I pleaded.

'I'll go and ask my manager,' the softly spoken woman responded, trying to be helpful. 'Could I have your name, please?'

When I didn't reply, she asked for my name again, louder now, and more audible to the other staff behind her at their desks. I had no choice but to bat on.

'Robert Tickner,' I said in muffled tones, looking down at my shoes and hoping no one else had heard.

She gave me an intrigued look, then quickly disappeared into a nearby office. I was hugely embarrassed to see a sudden flurry of activity at the back of the office, and then the manager himself came to the front counter, where I was still standing looking at my shoes some more.

'What can I do to help you, Mr Tickner?' he asked, clearly wanting to be helpful to a local MP, which had the unintended consequence of making me feel even more exposed and self-conscious.

'I was adopted, and I've come to ask what I need to do to lift the contact veto I lodged at this office a couple of years ago. I know it's a huge life step, but I think I'm ready to do it,' I blurted out.

The die had been cast.

The manager explained the detailed formalities of the

process. He also told me that counselling would be available at some future time to be arranged — apparently, this was the usual precursor to the lifting of a contact veto by an adopted person. But by the time he had finished speaking, I was much more in control of my feelings and confident that I knew what I was doing.

'Thanks for the offer, but I'm honestly sure I don't need counselling,' I assured him. 'I'm ready to proceed.'

Without any further delay, he organised the relevant documentation to lift the veto. I was grateful for his kindness.

In early December of 1992, I was ready for my next mission. I decided to lodge the application to seek out my original birth certificate, which would also reveal the name of my birth mother.

The day I made the decision, I was in Brisbane that morning, addressing a particularly volatile group of justifiably angry Aboriginal people in a large community meeting. They had come together to discuss Aboriginal deaths in custody and the follow-up to the government response to the Royal Commission. I had the job of coordinating the response across the country. These traumatised and grieving family members, whose kids, grandkids, or brothers had died in custody, were demanding answers as to why no one had been criminally charged by state and territory governments as a result of the deaths of their loved ones. Powerful and sometimes angry speeches were made by the grieving families, and, as was often the case in these meetings, tempers frayed and tears flowed. I didn't want to short-change anyone present or show anything other than the solidarity I felt, so I stayed until the meeting ran out of steam. Everyone had their say, and I responded to the concerns that had been raised.

Quickly gathering my things afterwards, I rushed for the waiting car, feeling that this could be one of the most important days of my life — setting the wheels in motion to get my birth certificate, no matter what. My problem was that I had such a narrow window of time in which to get back to Sydney and lodge the application: it was a Friday afternoon, I would be leaving Sydney again for some time on Sunday night, and I would be absent again in other parts of the country throughout the period leading up to Christmas. Today was my one opportunity for quite a while.

By the time I got to the airport in Brisbane, I had missed my Qantas plane, so I ran the full length of the terminal to see if I could catch an Ansett flight. It was a manic race to the gate, taking wrong turns, and even losing my way. But I got there.

Arriving in Sydney, I rushed like a man possessed to get to the Births Deaths & Marriages office in Ultimo before it closed at 4.00 pm. I arrived just in time, with only two minutes to spare. I hurriedly completed the documentation, and the pleasant and courteous young man behind the counter told me that my birth certificate would be available on 6 January.

I knew that the waiting time would feel like an eternity.

8

First steps towards
meeting my birth mother

I knew from the beginning that making contact with my birth mother was going to be a highly personal issue. There were likely to be considerable sensitivities around the meeting, and vulnerable people might be affected by my actions. It didn't for one moment cross my mind to make public the issues I was facing. The idea of making this a human-interest media story or to exploit it for political capital was anathema to me, and looking back I'm still so glad I respected the rights and interests of others. My adoption reunion was one of the best-kept secrets in Parliament House.

Finding time to seek out my birth parents was very challenging. As Jody would agree, I was a far-from-perfect partner, with my ministerial responsibilities taking me away from home for most of the year. When I was back in the electorate, I was totally immersed in the work required of a marginal seat, including a phenomenal level of engagement with almost every community group and school. I just gave it my all: I was fulfilling a lifelong dream to serve my community as their local federal MP, and had the added privilege of being an ALP minister in a portfolio I passionately believed in. My travel schedule was ridiculously demanding, and, for most of those six years, I worked almost a hundred hours over a seven-day week, and ran myself into the ground. In my view, the minister for Aboriginal and Torres Strait Islander affairs needs to be everywhere across this wide brown land, responding to invitations from Indigenous communities and leaders. But of course this meant that I had no real time to myself for my personal and family life.

Once, in the early days of my portfolio, before I got into my stride, my crazy travel schedule led me to make a fool of myself, much to the amusement of a local Aboriginal community — and much to my embarrassment. I had flown across Australia to the Kimberley area of Western Australia. I had visited six communities in one day, before finishing in Derby, where I opened a new Aboriginal-operated supermarket. I thought I'd made a great speech, and felt a sense of smug satisfaction that it had been captured by a visiting documentary film crew. My self-congratulatory mood soon wilted when one of my staff told me that when I'd cut the ribbon and declared the supermarket open, I had triumphantly proclaimed that 'this new venture will proudly serve the people of Broome for many years to come'. Broome was 220 km away. I recalled the quizzical looks the old Aboriginal stockmen of Derby had given me during the speech, and how the applause afterwards had been somewhat muted. I resolved never to make that mistake again.

The Tuesday after applying for my original birth certificate, I returned to my ministerial suite in Canberra and was welcomed, as always, by four Central Australian Aboriginal artefacts — snakes and lizards — spilling out of my office doors and looking as if they were about to escape into the corridors of the new Parliament House. They were placed there every morning, along with the Aboriginal and Torres Strait Islander flags and the Australian flag, and they were very precious to me — especially the two-metre-long, highly realistic snake, which lives with me to this day. My staff and I had set the office up this way to show we were open and engaged with the Indigenous community. Even Liberal and National Party members and senators welcomed the display as a refreshing change from the blandness of parliament, and many brought their guests around to my office to see the artefacts. That particular day, I passed the welcoming party of carved reptiles and greeted my team members in the front office. Taking a cursory look in my red message book, I saw a note to phone a Mr Barry Miles (not his real name) on a Sydney number. The words 'the application' jumped out at me, and a chill ran up my spine. One way or another, this was going to be a very important call.

I closed the door to my office to be by myself, and, within thirty seconds, I was on the phone to Mr Miles. He introduced himself as a senior staff member of the Registry of Births Deaths & Marriages, and told me in a calm and measured tone, 'I'm ringing you with some important news. I have your birth certificate in front of me.'

I audibly gasped, but let him go on.

'Your mother is still alive, but has lodged a contact veto,' he said.

I was mortified, and couldn't find the words to reply.

After a slight pause, he continued, 'However, this contact veto is not to deny future contact with you, but rather to have some control over the timing and manner of the contact.'

My spirits soared, but I was also in shock. I slumped back in my chair, then immediately bounded to my feet again, holding the phone to my ear and hanging on his every word as he continued to explain. He told me that my mother had written me a letter and gave me some information about the next steps. I can still so vividly remember that moment. It was unbelievably moving, and I felt privileged to be living through it. I was also deeply touched by the utterly professional and caring way that Mr Miles delivered the news.

For once in my life, I could barely string a sentence together. 'You don't know what this means to me,' I managed. 'You have touched me so deeply with this news. Is there anything more you can tell me?'

'Not now,' he said. 'You need to see the birth certificate for yourself and read the letter your mother has written to you.'

I promised to contact him as soon as possible to arrange to collect the birth certificate and the letter.

'You may wish to write a letter back to your mother, which will then be sent to her, if she wishes to receive it,' he concluded.

After I'd hung up the phone, I got up from my chair, opened my office door, and just stood there dumbstruck.

My trusted friend and colleague Di Hudson was sitting nearby.

'You won't believe the phone call I just had,' I told her. 'They've found my mother, and she's alive and wants to meet me. She knows nothing about me, but wants to meet me. There was a contact veto, but only to regulate contact, not to block me.'

Di knew that I'd applied for my birth certificate, and it was she who had put Mr Miles's message in the book, so she knew exactly what I was talking about. She was overjoyed for me, but I sensed she understood more sensitively than I did the challenges ahead. 'Don't rush it,' she advised me, as there were many issues yet to be worked through, and things could fall apart.

Still, I was stunned by the speed of events and by the magnitude of it all. I called Jody and immediately shared the news, but she and Di were the only people I told.

I was numbed by the news for some hours and, later, wandered the corridors of parliament in a daze. I am a very passionate person, but those passions and convictions are normally directed towards the interests of others. This, now, was an issue that affected me personally and deeply; it went to the core of my existence.

My next step was to make an appointment with Mr Miles to collect my birth certificate, but that was easier said than done. Parliament was sitting all the rest of that week, and then on Thursday, 13-year-old Jade was to fly to Canberra to meet up with me for a trip to Torres Strait for a major event on Friday. I had hardly spent any time with Jade, and so had sought special permission for her to travel with me. The only time I could arrange to meet with Mr Miles was on the Saturday night of our return to Sydney, and, due to my crazy schedule, he kindly made a special arrangement for me to collect the birth certificate from his home. Because of the sensitivity of the documentation, he thought it best not to post it to me.

Jade arrived on the Thursday and slept on the floor in my office until parliament rose in the early hours of Friday morning after a marathon session. I got a few hours of sleep in the office myself, and then at 7.00 am we flew out of Canberra on an air-force plane up to Weipa in Far North Queensland. From Weipa, we jumped on a small charter to Horn Island, and then travelled by boat to Thursday Island, where I was to attend a series of meetings with local community leaders who were advocating for a form of self-government for the Torres Strait Islands. The next day, Saturday, we flew to Melbourne where the land title of the former School of Army Health at Healesville was handed back over to Aboriginal ownership. Jade and I flew back to Canberra in the afternoon, where I collected my car and drove us to Stanwell Park. I dropped Jade at home, turned the car around, and drove to Sydney, arriving at close to 10.00 pm at the home of Mr Miles in the Eastern Suburbs.

At that time, I was driving my father's old Nissan Skyline, which had huge sentimental significance for me. The car was a link with my dad and mum, and it felt as if they were with me as I took this big step.

Stopping under a street lamp, I wrote a letter to my birth mother, as Mr Miles had suggested I could do. He had said the letter would be placed 'on the file', and would be available should my birth mother want to read it. I was intrigued by the fact that my mother and I already had our own file, and felt it must mean something encouraging.

I found it difficult to know what to write in this very first letter. I was in uncharted waters, and deeply conscious of the need to reassure her and give her the confidence to put her trust in me. Here is the letter I wrote under that street lamp, unfortunately in my terrible scrawl, and left with Mr Miles for transmission to my mother. I squibbed on the opening salutation; I simply didn't know how to address her. I also included a lot of identifying information, including my address and details of my work, none of which was passed on to her. This was because the adoption reunion process required such information to be shared in small steps, to protect the emotional wellbeing of both mother and child. Later, I was to learn of the grief caused by the rash actions of adopted children who confronted their birth parents without the support of expert guidance and mentoring.

19th December 1992
This is a letter I did not ever think I would write, only because I have had and still have a very wonderful life. I have always known I was adopted and it was never a

problem of any kind for me. I have never felt any kind of resentment towards you of any sort.

The main reason why I have never sought to make contact is that I am a rather sensitive soul and would never have done anything to hurt the feelings of my adopted mother and father.

Dad died 6 years ago, and two things have changed since then. One is that my adopted mother is now 80 and her memory is failing. She is still wonderful but needs help to live and is in hostel accommodation. The second is that I have a 10 week old son, Jack. These two events have drawn me to make contact with you.

I feel very positive about meeting you and I hope you feel the same way. I have no expectations and would not want to make you feel uncomfortable in any way, but feel it in my bones that we should meet.

You will know from my name that I am the Federal Minister for Aboriginal Affairs, and I hope that my public life does not put you off. I assure you that I am a very down to earth person, and my adoption and seeking to meet you is very special and private to me.

I lodged the form to get my birth certificate only a week ago, and was contacted by the Deputy Registrar of Births Deaths and Marriages, who has been very kind and allowed me to come to his house to collect the birth certificate. If you want to talk to him in confidence about anything I am sure it would be okay.

I don't know how long it will take the bureaucracy to get this letter to you but I hope it is not too long.

It is probably unlikely, but if you felt like getting together
on 24th December (my birthday), a special day for both of
us no doubt, it would be fine by me.

Alternatively, I will be back in Sydney in late December
or the New Year, and in the meantime can be contacted on
the phone numbers above.

Life is wonderful!!!

I hope to meet you soon.

I included a photograph of me, Jody, and Baby Jack in hospital, soon after Jack was born. Unfortunately, in my rush leaving Stanwell Park earlier that evening, I had inadvertently grabbed a photograph that didn't fully reveal my face.

Can you imagine my feelings of deep trepidation and fragility as I got out of my car at ten o'clock that Saturday night and walked to Mr Miles's front door with my handwritten letter? I was about to find out the name of my mother.

Mr Miles answered my knock and warmly welcomed me. I was full of apologies for being so late, but he told me not to worry. I think we may have gone inside his house briefly, but I was so nervous I don't remember. He handed me a brown envelope, which I knew contained my original birth certificate and the letter from my mother.

With only the dim veranda light to see by, I couldn't help peeking inside the envelope. There was the birth certificate, and there was the name of my mother: Maida Anne Beasley. The space left for my father's name was blank.

The name Beasley wasn't new to me. I remembered my mother saying it in one of the few childhood conversations

I could recall us having about my adoption. And there it was, right in front of me. I felt a rush of pride and admiration for my mum Gwen and her wisdom at being so open and honest about my adoption from the very beginning.

I could see the letter inside the envelope, too, but didn't look at it until I returned to my car. It was a short letter, written by hand on small pink-coloured writing paper. I climbed into the driver's seat and leant forward so I could read by the glow of the streetlight.

My mother also avoided a salutation at the start of her letter.

20-2-91 [I assume this was the day my mother lodged the contact veto]

My name is Maida Anne Kirwan (née Beasley).

I am your birth parent.

All my emotions are on the surface but I feel I must write to you.

You have always been in my thoughts, and the family who adopted you. They would give you the love and security of a family which I was not able to do.

Firstly, I must explain why my name is on the Contact Veto in case you feel you have been rejected by me. Please never feel that way. As some of my family still live in my home town I was concerned that any enquiries made locally may have become known to these people. My name is on the Adopted Contact Registrar. This means that if ever you would like to contact me you can do so direct and this would save you many hours of effort. May I ask that if you do decide to contact me, please do so by letter. I do not think I could handle a phone call or a sudden visit.

A few personal details of myself. Born in 1928 and keep good health. Am 5 feet and 8 inches tall with medium complexion, and I have an identical twin sister. My parents died of heart attacks. Father aged 69 and mother aged 67. I married in 1957 and have no children from this marriage.

My door will always be open to you.

Always in my heart.

Sincerely

Maida.

My head was a tangle of confused thoughts as I drove through the night back to Stanwell Park. Who was this woman who was my mother? What was her story? Was I made in her image? I still hadn't seen a photograph of her. Did we share the same kinds of feelings and values? And how would this reunion journey roll out, if, indeed, it proceeded at all? She might decide to back out, and if she did, there was nothing I could do.

Of course, these were all perfectly natural questions. There was still so much I didn't know. Her letter was loving and reassuring on some key issues, but it was also very short and didn't give a lot away.

9

Learning more about my birth mother

In a follow-up phone conversation, Mr Miles explained to me that another part of the Department of Community Services looked after and supported people who had chosen to proceed with an adoption reunion. I would be allocated a caseworker, he told me.

The next step was to arrange an appointment with my caseworker, Sandra (not her real name). We had our first meeting at the Department of Community Services' Parramatta office so that Sandra could teach me about the processes of the reunion. I'd had a simplistic assumption that I would be meeting my mother within days, but, after speaking to Sandra, I quickly realised this course of action would have been catastrophic for Maida. At that time, I couldn't conceive of her extremely fragile state or what an earth-shattering shock it had been for her when I made contact.

As far as my own feelings were concerned, it was relatively easy for me to progress the reunion, but I know for many other people who were adopted it has been much more difficult, and I feel for them. By the time I began the process, I felt comfortable in my skin, had been fortunate to have had a good life, and was lucky to have experienced some very privileged life opportunities. In every way, I was at peace with the world and my circumstances. My mother Maida, on the other hand, had lived a radically different life because of my adoption, and the steps towards our reunion would bring back much of the haunting pain of my birth and adoption.

It was a big moment when I met Sandra for the first time. I was very nervous, having never been in this kind of situation before: my life was now totally in the hands of a government official. I needn't have worried. Sandra welcomed me reassuringly in a kind and softly spoken manner, and I was immediately struck by her obvious intelligence and perceptiveness. Right from that very first meeting, we hit it off. I trusted her totally and was guided by her every step of the way. As our relationship developed, she taught me so much. Working to protect the interests of all parties involved in this reunion, she was always sensitive, supportive, and, importantly for me, right from the beginning had great patience in explaining to me how my mother was feeling. I often felt ashamed that I'd never had a proper understanding of the deep and ongoing grief that could be felt by a relinquishing mother.

Some details of our conversations are a bit blurred with the passing of the years, but some things I recall with crystal clarity. For example, when Sandra told me about her first contact with my mother, she said, 'She's a very special lady. I was touched by her. I don't think I've ever been more moved by anyone in this job.'

I learnt from Sandra of the mind-numbing shock Maida had experienced when Sandra first called, and then when a letter about our possible reunion arrived from the department that same day. She explained that my mother had kept the secret of my birth from all but the closest members of her family in the town of Orange, where I was conceived. She had come to Sydney to have her baby, and then later returned briefly to Orange with her terrible secret, which had dominated her entire life from then on. She had eventually married Greg Kirwan some five years later, but could never have children because of her fear that they would be taken away or in some way lost to her. This revelation, perhaps more than any other, rocked me to the core.

Sandra explained that the reunion process would be very controlled and taken step by step, and I came to see how important this was in giving my birth mother a greater sense of confidence and empowerment after the brutally disempowering experience of my forced adoption all those years ago. That process included the controlled sharing of personal details — Sandra hadn't yet told me where my mother lived or worked, for example.

Despite this care on Sandra's part, Maida blew her anonymity out of the water on my birthday, 24 December, when she sent a fax to my electorate office.

My electorate secretary, Anne Nichols, greeted me with a sheepish grin and said, 'There's an intriguing birthday message for you.'

Despite the close, almost family relationship I had with my electorate team, I hadn't yet shared the excitement of the unfolding adoption reunion. Anne must have thought I had a mystery romantic admirer when she thrust the fax into my hands.

It was a simple handwritten message: 'Happy birthday from Maida.'

Looking at the fax more closely, I assumed my mother must have been overwhelmed with excitement and tension when she sent it, as the top of the page recorded that it had come from Parramatta City Council. This must be where Maida worked. I sensed this was a breach of the adoption reunion protocols and immediately wondered what lay behind it, and if all was okay with her. At the same time, her message touched me deeply. I noticed that she had inadvertently reversed the fax numbers on her first try, and then had had to resend it. This has been a chronic problem of mine all my life, reversing numbers and letters, and I felt immediate solidarity with her.

I wondered whether the inclusion of Parramatta City Council's fax number was a code signal indicating that she wanted me to contact her. I phoned Sandra and explained what had happened and asked whether Maida wanted me to phone her. Sandra called Maida, and afterwards explained to me that the inclusion of the Parramatta City Council information had been a complete oversight by my mother in the excitement of sending the message. This was, after all, her first direct contact with me since the first week of my birth. Little wonder she would be nervous and on edge and not be thinking about what other information the fax was revealing.

The arrival of the fax was a prompt to me that it was time to break the news to my electorate staff, Anne, Margaret, and Noreen. Apart from anything else, I was busting to tell them about this unbelievable adventure I was living. I'd overheard them discussing the fax over morning tea, and one of them had even mentioned that she'd taken a call from a woman earlier in the day asking for my fax number. I was astounded, and also felt a bit cheated that someone in the office had spoken to my mother before me!

'Could you all please come upstairs for a moment?' I asked them. 'It'll only take a moment.'

We trekked up the stairs into a more formal private office, which was a rarefied zone of calm compared to the relentless pressures faced downstairs all day every day.

I began with, 'Take a seat. There's something I have to tell you,' and realised my mistake when I saw the blood drain from their faces. When an MP takes his key staff aside and commences a conversation like that, it invariably leads to a resignation or a confession of a political catastrophe of some kind.

'I have some extraordinary news, and I'm sorry I haven't been able to tell you before,' I added quickly.

'What is it?' Margaret asked nervously, almost at the same time as Anne said, 'What's happened? Has something gone wrong?'

Tears welled in my eyes, no doubt making them even more alarmed. 'I have a story to tell you,' I said. 'It's a very wonderful and uplifting story, and partly to do with the fax you were all talking about before. It was from my birth mother.'

I stopped then, because I needed a break to regain my composure. You could have heard a pin drop in the room.

These three women, who were like family to me, knew I was adopted. They thought the world of my mother Gwen, whom they'd met on several occasions when she'd come to Sydney. Now, they hung on every word as I told them in detail what had happened to me over the past three weeks, and the tears flowed freely from us all. Not much work was done for the rest of the afternoon by any of us, but thankfully it was Christmas Eve and the rest of the electorate already seemed to have started their holiday.

Sandra explained that the next step was for my mother and me to exchange letters and photographs — and this was where the challenges and complexities intensified. Jody, Jade, Jack, and I were spending Christmas in my mother Gwen's unit in Tuncurry, and so Sandra agreed to mail the very first photographs of Maida to me, care of the post office there.

We drove up on Christmas Day to start our holiday and to visit my mother Gwen in the aged-care residence around the corner. I was beside myself with the anticipation of getting the promised photographs, and could think of little else, despite the ongoing pressures of my ministerial role, which saw debate over Mabo issues extend into the Christmas break. The thought of such precious cargo winging its precarious way to me via Australia Post, incongruously sharing the mail van with thousands of Christmas cards and other assorted everyday cargo, was more than I could bear. I seriously considered calling Sandra to tell her I would drive back to Sydney to collect the photographs, but by then it was too late, as they'd already been posted.

On 30 December 1992, I went to the post office as planned to collect the expected mail and the very first photograph of my birth mother. The town was packed with tourists and locals going about their business, and there were long queues in the post office. People were buying stamps, lodging priority mail, and picking up business parcels, and it all seemed to take an inordinate length of time. Finally, I reached the counter.

One of my old school friends was standing there, and greeted me with, 'Hi Tick, what are you doing in town?'

'Just up to see my mum,' I said. 'I don't suppose there's a parcel here for me to collect?'

'Hang on, I'll check for you.' After what seemed like forever, she came back empty-handed. 'Nothing here, Tick, but there's some delays in the mail because of Christmas.'

I trudged mournfully back to the unit and called Sandra to chase the missing letter. She told me it was on its way, and now expected to arrive on New Year's Eve.

The following morning, I arrived at the post office as soon as the doors opened, and this time quickly took possession of a large brown envelope, which I knew had my mother's letter and photographs inside. I handled it reverently, like a sacred object. I was about to see the face of my mother for the very first time since I'd been taken from her as a tiny baby 40-plus years ago.

I didn't want to open the envelope on my own, so I rushed back to the unit and up two flights of stairs to be with Jade, Jody, and Baby Jack. I burst into the living room clutching the envelope, but suddenly felt overcome and daunted by the moment and needed encouragement from Jody and Jade to go through with opening the package.

We gathered around the dining-room table, with Jack crawling around the floor beside us, and I opened the envelope to see the face of my mother.

I stared and stared, unable to talk, just trying to cope with the magnitude of the moment.

It was a beautiful photograph of a very attractive woman looking up at the camera. She was smiling and bending over to look after a small child, who I learnt much later was the granddaughter of her twin sister.

Wishing the photograph would come to life, I stared at it for a long time. Her face held a sense of familiarity for me. There were my eyes looking back at me, and a striking resemblance in other features, too.

'She looks like you, Dad,' Jade said.

I immediately recognised where the photograph had been taken: Angel Place in Sydney, 50 metres from where I'd attended the Sydney University Liberal Club meeting and Malcolm Fraser's speech had propelled me into joining the ALP. Such a coincidence. I had thought about that meeting and place many times over the years, and about its contribution to shaping my path in life. There were some other photographs enclosed in the package, including photographs of her as a young schoolgirl in Orange.

Jade agreed to hand-make some special paper for me to use to write to my mother. She was always such a caring child and clearly understood the importance of making Maida feel welcome to our family. I was proud of her for the work and thought she put into this gesture; the paper she made was stunning.

And so, later that night, I poured myself a glass of wine and sat down at the dining-room table to write a long reflective letter to my mother Maida on Jade's paper. It was handwritten in my terrible script and, like all my letters, hard to read. But its saving grace was that it came from the heart. It was well after midnight by the time I finished writing.

1st January 1993

Dear Maida, Mother, Mum!!

How do I start this letter, what do I call you? That is only one of the many things we have to work out. I will abide by your wishes, but for my part, the fact is that you are my mother. Also I have always had a private disdain for the way some people call their mothers by their first name just to be smart. So IF and only IF you are comfortable I would like to think and speak of you as my mother. But if you would like me to call you Maida, it is okay with me too.

Be warned that this is unlikely to be a short letter as like you I am very emotional!!!

I do not feel afraid or nervous as you mentioned. I do, however, feel very excited and perhaps a little worried only because I want things to go so well as we both would hope. I am especially concerned that events unfold as YOU would want them to, and that you and Greg find your lives enriched, as we hope ours will be from meeting you.

Where do I begin?

Perhaps I should explain that there is another person I should immediately introduce you to and that is Jade, aged 13, whose dad I became when I married Jody 7 years ago. She made this paper at my request to start off this letter, and is very comfortable about these exciting developments. She has an obsession with horses and leases one, and she goes to Bulli High School. I wanted to write on this paper Jade made to show that she is with us in this exciting new adventure.

I should also apologise for my abysmal writing and spelling. My teachers used to say that I developed bad writing to cover up my bad spelling.

I explained how Jody and I had another child, too, Baby Jack, and as Jody was technically my first cousin, this meant that Jack was not only 'directly related to you as his Grandma, Nanna, etc. — you choose', he was also biologically related to mother Gwen, 'and this does make Jack a very special person before his life has even started'.

I had become increasingly conscious of Maida's vulnerability and fragility thanks to the discussions I had had with Sandra, which meant that now I wanted to try to build her trust and confidence in me — to reassure her that I had no issues of any kind with my adoption, and to make sure she knew how much I was looking forward to meeting her.

... let me make some things very clear because I think it is important to do so. In the period of my whole lifetime I have NEVER had any feeling of hostility or resentment whatsoever towards you. I emphasise this because I have read in some textbooks offering expert opinion that this may happen. Well, not for me! Never ever! I have nothing but positive feelings and expectations about meeting you and getting on well.

Why is this so? Two reasons, I think. (1) I have had such a good life. And (2) the approach my adopted Mum and Dad (whose names are Gwen and Bert) took to my adoption was very wise. I always knew I was adopted, and was told of the name Beasley and about being born in Crown Street Women's Hospital. Incidentally, I subsequently lived at 423 Crown Street, Surry Hills and represented that area as an Alderman on the Sydney City Council.

The second major thing I should make clear and emphasise is that you need have no fears whatsoever about meeting and all that we hope will flow from that. I cannot think of a single downside, except the fact that my public commitment to people and to politics will mean that sometimes I will have to be working when I would prefer to be talking to family or friends. I mention this only to let you know that I have a driving commitment to my beliefs and my political work. It is not about self-promotion or personal gain but is an innate motivation for my political values. I don't know where this comes from as Mum and Dad Tickner were not ALP supporters, although they were very caring about other people.

I reassured her that I would 'flow with your wishes absolutely on the question of when and where we should meet', and I added that no matter where we met, 'the event will be one of — if not the most — significant in our lives, as I am sure you will agree. Again, don't worry and don't be afraid. I will probably be unbelievably emotional no matter what we do beforehand. Just be yourself, and if we cry hopelessly then so what.'

I wrote about seeing her face for the first time in the photograph she sent me: '… with no exaggeration, opening the envelope was one of the most wonderful moments of my life. You look so good. So gentle.' I added, 'We look alike, especially when you were a school girl and I was just a lad.'

I told her how much I was looking forward to our meeting and joked about how nervous I was going to be about her safety until we met: '… be very careful crossing roads, getting out of bed, sneezing, or moving in any way. If anything should happen to your precious self I will never forgive you!'

I finished with what I hoped were encouraging words:

> *I already admire you so much and look forward to developing our friendship and understanding. I think we are both very lucky that this has happened to us. I have this overwhelming feeling that we should not waste a minute! I personally believe there was a one in one hundred thousand chance or less of us not liking each other. But Sandra's report of her meeting with you makes that less than one in a million. From what she has told me about you I am very proud that you are my mother … Take what time YOU need and*

do what is right for YOU. But above all else, feel proud,
confident, happy and as wonderful as I feel.

I had gone all out to convince her that I was totally free of
any possible anger or resentment towards her, and that it was
safe to meet me and to seek to build our relationship. I would
never let her down and wanted her to know this with all my
heart. Against these efforts, in my letter, I made a ham-fisted
blunder when I suggested a couple of possible places for our
first meeting: the Sydney Botanic Gardens or, unthinkingly,
out the front of the Crown Street Hospital where I'd been
born. I don't know what could have possessed me to say
something so utterly insensitive and stupid.

Without my knowing it, my letter contained another
dangerous bombshell. I had enclosed two photographs,
which, when my mother saw them, would inadvertently
endanger the whole process of reunion and even make her
doubt her sanity. To her, these photographs were a cruel
and deeply painful reinforcement of the suffering she had
experienced ever since losing her child.

The first photograph showed me, aged five or six, with
my grandmother Minnie Osborn on the front porch of 18
Lansdowne Street in Merrylands. This was the house where
my mum Gwen had grown up, and where Mum and Dad
had taken me as a baby immediately after my adoption
in 1951. I had noted the address on the back of the tiny
photograph.

In a coincidence that beggars belief, when my mother, in a state of great emotional vulnerability, received the photograph, she was sitting in her home just ten doors down, at number 38 Lansdowne Street. She had lived there since 1957, but had been visiting the site since 1955, when the land was first purchased. Greg Kirwan, her husband, was a carpenter and had built the house with his own hands — it remains there to this day. The coincidence was truly shocking. More likely than not, my mother would have been only ten houses away when the photograph was taken.

The second photograph was also extraordinary in its coincidence and must have deeply compounded the pain my mother felt. It was what I thought was a cute photograph of me, aged about four, sitting on Santa Claus's lap. My mother Gwen had told me it was taken at a department store in Parramatta, and the year, 1955, was clearly displayed on a big sign in the background. When Maida saw this photograph, she realised that she already had one very similar of her twin sister Cynthia's son, Daryl. When she rushed to look at it, she found it had been taken the same year as mine with exactly the same Santa. Even more disturbing for my mother was the fact that the department store was directly opposite the council building where she worked. She had been just a heartbeat away from me all those years ago.

When my mother learnt of these extraordinary coincidences in January 1993, they pushed her almost to the edge of a breakdown. Long after we met, she told me that when she saw the first photograph, she had run distraught from her house into Lansdowne Street — this woman who was so intensely private and had kept her terrible burdensome secret for so many years. She told me that she thought her mind was playing terrible tricks on her, or even that it might be some cruel current-affairs program hoax that would destroy her life.

Let's walk in my mother's shoes for a moment. She had given up her child back in December 1951, and had thought about what had become of him every single day of her life since. She couldn't bear to have any other children because of the pain of the forced adoption. She had only talked about this adoption with her husband, Greg, once in their 35 years of marriage.

Fast forward to January 1993, when my mother receives this letter and realises that the child she has grieved for so deeply, for so many years, was right under her nose: a little black-haired boy playing in her very street. It was just one more kick in the guts, pushing her pain to its limits. That pain must also have made her doubtful about how she might cope with the meeting I was proposing, and eroded her confidence that things could ever work out between us.

At the time I sent the letter, I knew nothing of these coincidences, of course, or this terrible new hurt that I had unintentionally inflicted. It fell to Sandra to tell me what had happened and to talk my mother through the avalanche of pain that had come with the rekindled sadness and loss of the last 40 years.

10

Adoption practices in New South Wales in the 1950s

Most people born after 1970 would find it almost inconceivable that less than 20 years earlier, a 22-year-old woman, as my mother was, living with her family in country New South Wales could have been turned out by her father because she had conceived a child outside of marriage. At that time, it was seen as so shameful that keeping the child was usually impossible. Not only was there no supporting parents' benefit, but the social marginalisation of single mothers, including by their own families, was all pervasive.

This wasn't a social stigma confined to Australia. The Canadian singer-songwriter Joni Mitchell, who relinquished her child for adoption in the late 1960s and was reunited with her in the 1990s, described the scandal of conceiving a child outside marriage as being so intense, even in the late 1960s, that it was 'like you murdered someone'.

I learnt not to ask my mother about the details of what

happened to her in Crown Street Hospital in December 1951, or what it was like for her in the months leading up to my birth and subsequent adoption. It was made clear to me, by her and Sandra, that the events of that time were simply too painful for my mother to talk about to anyone. But it is beyond doubt that, after she became pregnant, my mother was unable to continue to live in the family home or the town where she had grown up and to which the Beasley family had contributed over many decades. I never knew my grandfather Clifton Ernest Havelock Beasley personally, but I later learnt from my mother's husband, Greg, that he was a hard, gruff, and at times even cruel man, although not violent. There is no doubt in my mind that he was one of the primary reasons my mother was forced to leave Orange after I was conceived. Having been born in 1891 and served in WWI, he was of course a man from another era, and no doubt his views would have reflected that time.

I also know that my mother showed strong feelings of hostility whenever Crown Street Hospital was mentioned. We now know from many formal reports and the evidence from mothers and hospital staff given in government inquiries that the practices of the hospital were often cruel and damaging to the single women who went there to give birth. While the practices were not uniform around Australia and varied within states, it was very common for unmarried mothers in hospitals to be stigmatised, disparaged, and treated very differently from married women. The files of unmarried mothers were marked 'baby for adoption' or 'BFA', and there is considerable evidence that nursing staff often displayed disdain towards those women. In some hospitals, there is evidence that unmarried mothers were given sedatives and drugs to inhibit milk production. Although in the early 1950s the prevailing practice in many hospitals was not to have children with their mothers in the ward, in the case of mothers of children marked for adoption, there was a strong practice of denying contact altogether or limiting contact in the belief that this would somehow reduce the grief of the mother following the loss of her baby to adoption. Some hospital nurses from this time have expressed remorse about their role in the implementation of this practice because of the permanent damage it causes to the mothers.

My own mother simply refused to talk about these things. She was a closed book whenever I sought to know more about her experience in the hospital or at the accommodation she lived in during those pregnant months in Sydney, far from her family and friends in Orange. What I know from her demeanour and manifest sadness was that it was a grim and deeply unhappy period of her life, which left brutal scars on the core of her being.

Long after we eventually met, I became aware that Maida was following closely the work of the Parliament of New South Wales Legislative Council Standing Committee on Social Issues, which in 1998 was given the reference to conduct a wide-ranging inquiry into adoption practices in New South Wales from 1950 until 1998. The committee had the authority to inquire into and report on the administrative practices in those adoptions and whether they involved unethical and unlawful practices. The committee was also asked to advise the government on what policies should be adopted to deal with the distress caused to people by these former policies.

I would like to acknowledge the incredible courage of the women whose political actions, lobbying, and legal actions contributed to persuading the government of the day to refer this matter to the Parliamentary Committee. The courage of these woman has left a lasting legacy.

The committee was chaired by Labor MLC Jan Burnswoods (an old friend of mine), and it reported on 8 December 2000. The next day, 9 December (Maida's birthday), the Sydney media reported the outcome of the committee's deliberations. It delivered wide-ranging recommendations, including recommendation 16, which stated, 'The NSW Government should issue a statement of public acknowledgment that past adoption practices were misguided, and that, on occasions, unethical or unlawful practices may have occurred causing lasting suffering for many mothers, fathers, adoptees and their families.' The next recommendation called on 'departments, private agencies, churches, hospitals, professional organisations, and individuals involved in past adoption practices [to be] encouraged to issue a formal apology to the mothers, fathers, adoptees and their families who have suffered as a result of past adoption practices'.

Following the inquiry, it took until 2012 for the New South Wales parliament to pass a formal apology for forced adoption practices, which it did on 20 September, two months after my mother Maida had passed away. This New South Wales apology was preceded by an apology from the parliament of Western Australia in 2010, and accompanied in 2012 by apologies from all other states and territories, except the Northern Territory, which followed in 2013.

A very large number of people were affected by these events; the number of adoptions just between 1951 and 1975 totalled an estimated 150,000 babies. It has been further estimated that the total number of adoptions Australia-wide from the 1940s to the new millennium may have been as high as 250,000.

At the national level, in November 2010, following on from the Western Australian apology, the Senate referred an inquiry into former forced-adoption policies and practices to the Community Affairs References Committee. The committee reported in February 2012, and the report included extensive recommendations, including a call for a formal apology by the national government. The Senate committee concluded that it was 'incontrovertible that forced adoption was common' and occurred when children were given up for adoption because their parents, particularly their mothers, were forced to relinquish them or faced circumstances in which they were left with no other choice. I have no doubt that my own mother felt that she had no choice but to have me adopted.

The peak of adoptions in Australia actually occurred in the period 1971–72 — almost 10,000 babies were adopted in that year — and then began to fall quite quickly. The Senate committee observed that this coincided with the decline in births amongst women generally and noted that there were a range of possible causes for the decline, including the legalisation of abortion and the widespread introduction of family planning and contraception advice. It is also the case that the proportion of adoptions to births has decreased since the 1970s, due to the increased social acceptance of single-parent families and de facto relationships. Contrary to popular mythology, which I had not appreciated, the introduction of the supporting mother's benefit by the Whitlam government did not occur until two years after the rate of adoption started to plummet.

Reading the Senate committee report is also very helpful to understanding the changing social attitudes towards adoption in post–World War II Australia. Prior to World War II, there had been a move away from the institutionalisation of children towards the option of adoption, and, following the end of the war, there developed the 'clean break' theory, as described in the report:

> Developmental psychologists premised their beliefs on the long-held notion that a child is a 'blank slate' as a newborn. They argued that the personality and intelligence of an individual is determined by environment, not genetics. The prevailing theories advocated that the psychological and financial qualifications of a married couple were superior to those of single mothers and impoverished families. Therefore, placing the child in an adoptive home within the earliest possible timeframe was the primary way of safe-guarding the welfare of the child.

I guess my life was hugely impacted by this view of the world, but sure as hell my adoption reunion has proven to me beyond doubt, and contrary to my expectations, that I was in no way a 'blank slate' when I was born.

The Senate committee's research and observations showed a deep prejudice against single mothers at that time, including from doctors, and that prejudice continued unabated for at least two further decades after I was born. One doctor from the children's department of the Prince of Wales Hospital, Doctor Grunseit, wrote in 1973 in *The Medical Journal of Australia*, 'In New South Wales most unmarried mothers ... are more likely to be poor, undernourished and of low intelligence, if not actually retarded.' Such attitudes are repugnant, but they do help to explain why so many women were so unjustly treated over so many decades.

The Senate committee also reported that another doctor at the Royal Women's Hospital in Melbourne, Doctor Lawson, gave a public address in 1959, which was quoted in *The Medical Journal of Australia*, and stated, 'The prospect of the unmarried girl or of her family adequately caring for a child and giving it a normal environment and upbringing is so small that I believe for practical purposes it can be ignored. I believe that in all such cases the obstetrician should urge that the child be adopted ... The last thing that the obstetrician might concern himself with is the law in regard to adoption.' As I see it, the rights and concerns of vulnerable young women meant nothing to people like this, and they displayed a disdain and arrogance that knew no bounds.

On the other side of the equation, there was a huge demand from childless couples for children they could adopt. By the 1950s, according to the Senate committee report, there were more couples wishing to adopt a child than mothers wishing to relinquish their child.

The committee also reported on the experience of forced adoption and how it could push mothers towards suicide or suicidal feelings. These risks were further exacerbated by the inability of so many women to talk about the adoption and the child they had relinquished, often in awful circumstances. In the words of the report, 'The culture of secrecy that surrounded adoption throughout the period in which the clean break theory was prominent meant women carried their experience as a secret from even their closest friends and families.' This was my own mother's story and her life for over 40 years.

I will let one of the witnesses to the Senate committee speak her words on these pages, as they seem to me to capture the rage of my mother, which was mostly unspoken, but which I knew was only just below her skin and ready to erupt in private and away from the prying eyes of the rest of the world — including me. While my mother had a different direct experience to the person quoted, I think that she would share the deep anger at the 'obscene prejudice' displayed towards unmarried mothers of the time.

The Senate witness June Smith is quoted in the committee report as championing the importance of public recognition of past events. She said,

We need to be respected in this country's history as mothers who had their babies taken forcibly from them for no other reason than to satisfy the ideals of others. We need to be respected in this country's history as mothers who were unjustly abused, betrayed and punished by all governments, hospital staff, welfare workers, religious hierarchies and society because of their inhumane, obscene prejudice towards us.

Arguably the most detailed and informative research undertaken into the impact of adoption was the National Research Study on the Service Response to Past Adoption Practices. This study was commissioned by the Community and Disability Services Ministers' Conference (a national meeting of federal and state and territory ministers) and the federal Department of Families, Housing, Community Services and Indigenous Affairs as it then was. It was publicly released in August of 2012, shortly after Maida's death, and was partly based on direct surveys of parents whose babies were adopted (overwhelmingly the mothers, who numbered 505) as well as 823 adopted individuals. It complements the Senate committee report, and preceded the national apology, which was given the next year.

Firstly, the study concluded that 'there were very few birth mothers in the study who felt that the adoption was their choice', and that 'the most commonly identified contributing factors to their child's ultimate adoption were family pressure and/or lack of family support, and mothers often talked about emotions such as grief, loss, shame and secrecy surrounding their experiences'. The study further concluded, 'Mental health and wellbeing measures used in the survey indicate a higher than average likelihood of these mothers suffering from a mental health disorder compared to the general population, with close to one-third of the mothers showing a likelihood of having a severe mental disorder at the time of survey completion. Mothers rated lower quality of life satisfaction than the Australian norm, and over half had symptoms that indicate the likelihood of having post-traumatic stress disorder.'

These are incredible findings, but I doubt they would have shocked my mother. I saw time and again how her deep stress and distress manifested, often triggered by adoption-related reminders, such as old photographs or conversations. Those who knew Maida could see her pain, but the way she handled it made me realise that she had become a master of cover-up and self-protection. She did this by internalising her anger and anxiety on almost all occasions, but I could still see the underlying grief and distress that permeated her life.

The national research study also reported comprehensively on the situation of persons who were adopted — my category. I was eager to look at these results as soon as I gained access to the report. I know that I am in the minority of adoptees, for reasons I think have been made clear in my writing, but I have been deeply interested in the situation and circumstances of other adopted people as I have passed through my life. I have often reached out to adopted people that I have come across, especially where I have been able to assist them with thoughts about potential family reunion or relations with their birth family. I have assisted a number of people in this situation, including a former colleague, who I managed to encourage to link up with her very well-known birth father and mother.

This said, I cannot emphasise strongly enough that I also know many individual adopted people whose lives were irretrievably damaged by their adoption and their ill-fated attempts to make contact with their birth mother. I know people who have made initial contact with their birth mother or father only to find that they are unable to sustain the relationship for some reason. And I know those who have attempted to contact their birth mother, only to be met with a wall of rejection, and even outright hostility.

From the birth-mother perspective, I have been told on good authority by a departmental source that there have been many examples of mothers who experienced extreme traumatic feelings of grief and anxiety when they were advised that their child wanted to make contact with them. Their secret might have been kept from husbands and other children for decades, and the rest of the family might have had no idea that their wife and mother ever had another child who had been relinquished for adoption. The complexity and challenges of adoption reunions is further tragically demonstrated by the fact that some of these women experience suicidal thoughts and some of them have sadly taken their own lives.

On the other side of the equation, I have dealt with adopted people who have refused to have any contact with their birth family, despite attempts by their mothers to establish contact with them. Others have permitted initial contact, but then broken off the relationship, which must seem like a nightmare revisited for those birth mothers who suffer the double whammy of loss of the child at birth and then the rejection in later life.

Human relationships are complex, and I do not make any judgements here: reunions are hard and challenging for both mother and child, and can be tough on the wider adopted family as well. Sensitive and respectful processes were put in place with the creation of the reunion laws, which, if followed, give the best prospects for successful reunions to occur. It must be clearly understood that the great gift I was given in the success my own adoption reunion story is relatively rare. There is good reason for this, which is that many adopted people, as well as birth mothers, were damaged by the adoption.

When I read the statistics of the national research study, I was not surprised to read of the findings related to adoptees and the conclusion that 'One of the most significant findings within this respondent group appears to be that, regardless of whether they had a positive or more challenging experience growing up within their adoptive family (roughly equal proportions of each participated in this study), most participants identified issues relating to problems with attachment, identity, abandonment and the parenting of their own children.' Even though the statistics are arguably more ambivalent and far less alarming than the figures demonstrating the impact of forced adoption on relinquishing mothers, they are nonetheless serious cause for concern.

The study further concluded that 'Compared to Australian population estimates, adoptees responding to our survey had lower levels of wellbeing and higher levels of psychological distress, and that almost 70% of adoptee survey respondents agreed that being adopted had resulted in some level of negative effect on their health, behaviours or wellbeing while growing up.' These feelings included hurt concerning the 'secrecy and lies' surrounding their adoption and a 'subsequent sense of betrayal', as well as feelings of abandonment, low levels of self-worth, and difficulties in forming attachments to others.

I did not participate in this survey, but, had I done so, I would have been in the remaining 30 per cent, who did not experience these feelings. That doesn't mean that I don't feel great empathy and compassion for those who suffered as a result of their adoption, and I acknowledge and deeply respect the suffering of those who did not share my experience. How could it be otherwise?

I am in the minority in the group of adoptees for another reason as well. The national research study reported that 60 per cent of the people surveyed had had some form of contact with their mothers, but only 45 per cent of that number (i.e., less than 30 per cent of the total participants) described a relationship that was ongoing. Further, the study found that around 25 per cent of the total number surveyed had had some contact with their fathers, but only one half of those (i.e., around 13 per cent of the total number) had ongoing contact. Given that I had huge ongoing contact with my mother from the time of meeting her until her passing, and also full-on expansive contact with my father and my brothers and sisters since the time of the first meeting, clearly I am in a very distinct and even tiny minority. I consider myself to be immensely and deeply privileged that I have known the love of three families, and each of them has been and remains hugely important, influential, and special to me in my life. I honour them and rejoice in their love and companionship and the contribution each and every one of them has made to my life.

The national research study did not have a large sample of adopting parents participate in the survey: the number was only 94, compared with the significantly larger sample size of the other surveyed groups I have mentioned. Drawing conclusions from this data would therefore appear to be more problematic, but there does appear to be a well-founded conclusion that most adopted parents were satisfied with the initial adoption process and, in the longer term, that, by mental-health and wellbeing measures, the adopting parents fared better than other affected groups surveyed.

I have recounted these findings of the national research study in order to convey some impression of the overall societal impact of the adoption processes, which by any measure had an immense and adverse impact on close to half a million Australians who have lived in my lifetime, even on a conservative estimate.

For all those mothers, and the others who shared their pain, the national apology moved in the Parliament of Australia on 21 March 2013 by Prime Minister Julia Gillard was of some comfort. I welcomed that apology, too, and know that, had my mother Maida lived to hear it, she also would have deeply appreciated it.

The words of the motion of the apology adopted by the Australian parliament on 21 March 2013 read as follows:

National Apology for Forced Adoptions

1. Today, this Parliament, on behalf of the Australian people, takes responsibility and apologises for the policies and practices that forced the separation of mothers from their babies, which created a lifelong legacy of pain and suffering.

2. We acknowledge the profound effects of these policies and practices on fathers.

3. And we recognise the hurt these actions caused to brothers and sisters, grandparents, partners and extended family members.

4. We deplore the shameful practices that denied you, the mothers, your fundamental rights and responsibilities to love and care for your children. You were not legally or socially acknowledged as their mothers. And you were yourselves deprived of care and support.

5. To you, the mothers who were betrayed by a system that gave you no choice and subjected you to manipulation, mistreatment and malpractice, we apologise.

6. We say sorry to you, the mothers who were denied knowledge of your rights, which meant you could not provide informed consent. You were given false assurances. You were forced to endure the coercion and

brutality of practices that were unethical, dishonest and in many cases illegal.

7. We know you have suffered enduring effects from these practices forced upon you by others. For the loss, the grief, the disempowerment, the stigmatisation and the guilt, we say sorry.

8. To each of you who were adopted or removed, who were led to believe your mother had rejected you and who were denied the opportunity to grow up with your family and community of origin and to connect with your culture, we say sorry.

9. We apologise to the sons and daughters who grew up not knowing how much you were wanted and loved.

10. We acknowledge that many of you still experience a constant struggle with identity, uncertainty and loss, and feel a persistent tension between loyalty to one family and yearning for another.

11. To you, the fathers, who were excluded from the lives of your children and deprived of the dignity of recognition on your children's birth records, we say sorry. We acknowledge your loss and grief.

12. We recognise that the consequences of forced adoption practices continue to resonate through many, many lives. To you, the siblings, grandparents, partners and other family members who have shared in the pain and suffering of your loved ones or who were unable to share their lives, we say sorry.

13. Many are still grieving. Some families will be lost to one another forever. To those of you who face the

difficulties of reconnecting with family and establishing ongoing relationships, we say sorry.

14. We offer this apology in the hope that it will assist your healing and in order to shine a light on a dark period of our nation's history.

15. To those who have fought for the truth to be heard, we hear you now. We acknowledge that many of you have suffered in silence for far too long.

16. We are saddened that many others are no longer here to share this moment. In particular, we remember those affected by these practices who took their own lives. Our profound sympathies go to their families.

17. To redress the shameful mistakes of the past, we are committed to ensuring that all those affected get the help they need, including access to specialist counselling services and support, the ability to find the truth in freely available records and assistance in reconnecting with lost family.

18. We resolve, as a nation, to do all in our power to make sure these practices are never repeated. In facing future challenges, we will remember the lessons of family separation. Our focus will be on protecting the fundamental rights of children and on the importance of the child's right to know and be cared for by his or her parents.

19. With profound sadness and remorse, we offer you all our unreserved apology.

I think my mother Gwen would have found some of the language of the apology challenging, as did some other adopting parents, judging by media reports of their responses. Maybe I'm just too close to it, but I can't find it in my heart to apportion any level of blame to my mother Gwen or my father Bert for the loss suffered by my mother Maida. And I know from many conversations with Maida that she had nothing but respect and appreciation for the role my mother Gwen and father Bert played in my life, and, without any attempt to gain favour with me, soon after we met, she quietly placed a photograph of Bert and Gwen in the living room at 38 Lansdowne Street.

I don't want to suggest for one moment that there weren't adopting parents who treated their adopted children cruelly, or others who hid the fact of the adoption from their child or children and thereby potentially further contributed to the trauma of the adoption, or indeed inadvertently created such trauma by their actions. Despite this, my sense, from all that I've read and observed on this issue to date, is that most adopting parents were well-intentioned and genuinely wanted to give a home to a child.

This doesn't mean that closed adoption as it was carried out over those decades was good public policy. I welcomed and supported the national apology, and all the state and territory apologies, each as an important act of respect, atonement, and social justice for those affected Australian women and their children. It is critical to understand this complex, deeply distressing dimension of the social history of our country from the perspective of the mothers who had to give up their children and who might not have seen them again for decades, or indeed ever.

There is a postscript to all of this for me. During my time as CEO of Red Cross, I became heavily involved in the support of a program called the Young Parents Program, which was designed specifically to support the needs of young women and men up to the age of 25 years, and which is still running today. Through the program, young parents are able to access the safety, security, and support they need to help them with parenting. The program overwhelmingly benefits young single female teenage parents, focusing on their empowerment and on increasing their capacity for education and employment. The program has been evaluated on numerous occasions, and during 2013–14, for example, 95 per cent of all participants, all of whom had entered the program because they risked having their child removed from their care, were able to ensure that they kept their children, through the parenting and essential life skills and attributes they learnt in the program.

Of course, I had both an emotional and an intellectual commitment to this work. At a major fundraiser for the program held at the Bondi Pavilion in 2013, soon after my mother's death, I spoke out as an adopted person, urging public financial support for the program. My experience has been that in a large general audience of 200 or so people, there are likely to be at least a few people touched by adoption. Sure enough, at this function, after I had finished speaking publicly about my own adoption experience for the first time, a number of women unrelated to one another came forward to shed some tears and to thank me for the openness and honesty of my story. They all pleaded for support for the young mothers benefiting from the program. I have always been inspired by the young women participating in this and similar programs — by their determination to do the right thing by their kids and to seize new life opportunities, sometimes after having endured the school of hard knocks in their family and personal lives. In previous decades, those same inspiring young women would have had their children taken from them.

11

The Stolen Generations

I have thought long and hard about whether I should include anything in this book about the Stolen Generations, who have a fundamentally different story. Their story is about the racist assimilationist practices that underpinned the separation of Aboriginal children from their families over many generations. On balance, I have decided to do so, because there is the huge common thread in the pain of mothers, and no story about adoption in Australia would be complete without due reference and respect being paid to the tens of thousands of Aboriginal and Torres Strait Islander people who were taken from their mothers, and to the loss and pain of the mothers themselves, their families, and the wider Aboriginal and Torres Strait Islander community. It was also a period of appalling government policy, the aftermath of which I had much to do with in my time as minister for Aboriginal and Torres Strait Islander affairs.

In the case of Aboriginal and Torres Strait Islander mothers whose children were stolen from them, very different government policies prevailed to the adoption policies I have written about in the preceding pages. These other policies gave rise to what we as Australians know to be the Stolen Generations. Their litany of suffering was chronicled in the *Bringing Them Home* report of the Australian Human Rights Commission.

The public call for this inquiry was one of my most important actions as a minister, and was advocated at a time during which my own life was in such huge turmoil because of the adoption reunion process. It was at a time when my own birth mother was living in a precarious emotional state, as she sought to come to terms with being reunited with her own son after 41 years of separation. And it was at a time when I was right in the middle of the process of meeting my birth father, his wife, Lola, and my sisters and brothers.

My own adoption reunion, and my personal life more generally, frequently overlapped with my public life in the Indigenous-affairs portfolio. Thus, the personal overlapped with the political, and I have to believe that overlap helped to positively shape and reinforce the public policy outcomes — at least in a modest way.

There is always a challenge as a government minister in the Indigenous-affairs portfolio to adhere to the principles of cabinet government, while still fulfilling your obligations and the expectations of Aboriginal and Torres Strait Islander people, who see the minister as their advocate in government and in public debate. I fully admit that I pushed the boundaries of that relationship the whole time I was minister. In order to achieve changes and advances in public policy, I had to frequently speak out on issues in order to win the hearts and minds of the public and thus, by getting the community behind me, to help influence the shaping of public policy. I did this on all the big issues of the day: the establishment of the reconciliation process; the fight for a just Native Title Act; the establishment of the Indigenous Land Fund; the creation of the office of the Aboriginal and Torres Strait Islander Social Justice Commissioner; and, as I will describe here, the creation of the Stolen Generations Inquiry.

My interest in what happened to the Stolen Generations went way back. I had first become aware of the issues when I worked as a volunteer for the Aboriginal Legal Service in the early 1970s, soon after my graduation as a lawyer. As an adopted person, I was naturally drawn to this issue, but at first had no idea of the extent to which the policies of separation had become an enshrined practice of government across Australia.

In June of 1978, I went on a holiday to the Northern Territory with my mother and father, driving up in the family car to Central Australia. During that trip, I bought a book in a service station that changed my life. *A Bastard Like Me* by Charlie Perkins told the story of Charlie's life up until that time. Charlie had risen to lofty heights in the public service, while still retaining the mindset of an agitator — a mindset that I came to know and respect in my own extensive direct contact with him over future years. Little did I know that within six years of my having read the book, I would be calling out to Charlie Perkins from inside a paddy wagon in front of the New South Wales Parliament House, having been arrested for allegedly pulling down the Parliament House fence in an Aboriginal land rights demonstration.

It was Charles Perkins's description in his book of the experiences of his people in Central Australia that moved me so deeply:

> If tribal people were living around the towns, on cattle stations or near settled places, permanently resident there, the police would just whip them off, no trouble. Children were the main victims of this division of families. The troopers would ride up and say, 'All right, get the half-caste kids!' Like rounding up the lambs from the rest of the sheep, they would separate them, put them in a truck and off they would go. These kids were brought up in institutions across the Territory. That is why a lot of us have hang-ups. How else could it be? You miss the love of a mother and all the other things that go with it, the family circle. As a young kid, four or five years old, dumped with a lot of strangers, you can be emotionally scarred for life.

I can remember how reading this for the first time affected me. There was not the slightest hint of my own personal situation in this; I was empathising with the loss that had been suffered by others, and not by me. But the memory of Charlie's book stuck with me as I left my secure academic position and went to work for the Aboriginal Legal Service on a full-time basis in late 1978, where I would stay for the next six years until I was elected to the House of Representatives in the by-election in March 1984. Another work that increased my awareness and understanding of the Stolen Generations was Professor Peter Read's landmark work *The Stolen Generations*, which has received justified praise. Peter's book was published in 1981, and, the year before, Peter and a friend of mine, the late Oomera (Coral) Edwards, had established the first Link-Up organisation — a service to help the Stolen Generations trace their families.

I was deeply involved in all the big issues in the Indigenous-affairs portfolio during the 1980s, when I was still a backbench member. Then, following the 1990 federal election, Bob Hawke appointed me as the minister for Aboriginal and Torres Strait Islander affairs, and one of my first major challenges in that role was to coordinate the national response to the Royal Commission into Aboriginal Deaths in Custody. During that time, Lowitja (Lois) O'Donoghue, the chair of the board of the Aboriginal and Torres Strait Islander Commission, confided in me that she had been one of the children taken from their mothers.

One of the outcomes of our work on this Royal Commission response was that national and coordinated funding was provided for Link-Up organisations Australia-wide. As a result, the level of public awareness and public understanding of the Stolen Generations issues expanded enormously, and valuable work could be done in communities with the new funding.

Later, in 1992, I was sitting beside Paul Keating in the Redfern sun when he stepped forward to make the now famous Redfern Park speech. In that speech, he stated simply, 'We took the children from their mothers.' These words were a brief but powerful acknowledgment of what had occurred, words that resonated around the world.

I was very conscious at the time that there were calls for some kind of further inquiry into the practices and policies that had led to the Stolen Generations, including calls from the Secretariat of National Aboriginal and Islander Child Care (SNAICC). Unfortunately, there was no interest elsewhere in government for such a further inquiry, and there was not enough ongoing pressure on the government for this to occur.

By 1994, the government was starting to feel the toll of the battles that had been fought for Aboriginal and Torres Strait Islander rights during that term of government. It was with this background that, on 3 October 1994, I went to Darwin for a magnificent event organised by Aboriginal people, which I think helped to change the course of Australian history. The conference in Darwin was called the Going Home Conference. It was a big event of some 600 Aboriginal and Torres Strait Islander people who had been affected by the government policies of removal of children from families. They came together to discuss compensation, access to archives, and related issues.

I went to that event with a steely resolve to show some leadership on the issue of the call for a public inquiry, which I thought could be of enormous value to the nation and provide some relief and justice for those who had suffered so much. I told the trusted team in my office of my proposal to support the call for an inquiry, and they worked on some ideas with me, but I did not talk in advance to any other minister, or even to my colleagues in the Aboriginal and Torres Strait Islander community (including Lowitja O'Donoghue), as I wanted it to be a surprise. My ministerial-office colleagues and I developed the idea that a useful vehicle for a potential inquiry could be the Human Rights Commission, and we decided that I would write to the attorney-general on this issue and directly take up the idea with the commission. We prepared a media release, and every line of it was workshopped to make sure we got it right.

I knew that I was sticking my neck out when I rose to speak at the Darwin conference, but I remember being very sure that what I was doing was right.

I issued my media release, in which I said of removing Indigenous children from their families that 'although the practice has been long discredited there are many matters associated with it which remain unresolved and in need of attention' and that 'there would be considerable merit in a comprehensive analysis of matters associated with the practice'. Such an analysis, I said, 'would be useful in giving the wider community a better understanding of the massive human hardship inflicted on Aboriginal people by family separations ... and the consequences which continue to be felt'.

I concluded by saying that a national analysis of the practice of family separations 'may well have an important role in the process of reconciliation between Aboriginal and Torres Strait Islander people and the wider community, but how it could be conducted and by whom remains to be determined'. I promised to hold discussions with the attorney-general Michael Lavarch, the Aboriginal and Torres Strait Islander Commission, Aboriginal and Torres Strait Islander Social Justice Commissioner Mick Dodson, and the state and territory ministers for Aboriginal and Torres Strait Islander affairs. I issued letters to them contemporaneously with the Darwin speech.

Michael Lavarch, who was then the attorney-general, is a highly principled person, who I admire greatly, and he was very supportive of the proposal. He took the opportunity for advancing the idea in the government's 'Justice Statement' in May 1995, and, with his agreement, I announced that the President of the Human Rights and Equal Opportunity Commission, Sir Ronald Wilson, together with Mick Dodson, would head a national inquiry into the formal practice: the Stolen Generations Inquiry.

I do not intend to write here about the political developments that occurred subsequent to the tabling of the final report of the commission, which was titled *Bringing Them Home*, and which was finally released in 1997, during the period of the Howard government. It was and remains a matter of genuine sadness to me that Prime Minister Howard did not issue the apology that was called for in the report. I have praised John Howard for his role on other issues, including gun control and independence for Timor-Leste, but on this one, I think he made a mistake. Other recommendations in the report got lost as the political focus and pressure for an apology became the cause célèbre of many in the nation.

When the apology was finally given by Prime Minister Kevin Rudd, it was supported by the opposition leader, Brendan Nelson, and carried with the support of substantially the whole parliament. It was a great day for Australia.

I was given a ticket to attend the apology by the staff of the minister for Indigenous affairs, Jenny Macklin. Arriving late on a flight from Melbourne, I finally made it to the last remaining place I could find — a remote seat in the very back row of the gallery, three storeys up, behind some glass panelling. The seat was made better by the fact that I bumped into my former flatmate, and former deputy chair of ATSIC, Sol Bellear, and we savoured the moment together on that very back bench of the public gallery.

The commentator Robert Manne wrote in 2001, 'No inquiry in recent Australian history has had a more over-whelming reception nor, at least in the short term, a more culturally transforming impact.' I never had the slightest doubt about the impact the inquiry would have on our country; I knew the outcome would be a huge step forward in coming to terms honestly with our own history as a nation.

So how many Indigenous mothers and families had been impacted by this practice instituted by governments throughout much of the 20th century? The *Bringing Them Home* report finishes saying, 'Nationally we can conclude with confidence that between one in three and one in ten

Indigenous children were forcibly removed from their families and communities in the period from approximately 1910 until 1970. In certain regions and in certain periods the figure was undoubtedly much greater than one in ten. In that time not one Indigenous family has escaped the effects of forcible removal … Most families have been affected, in one or more generations, by the forcible removal of one or more children.'There, in plain words, is the horrific scale of the damage of these policies to many thousands of mothers, children, and their families.

For those who wish to know and understand more about what occurred, I commend the many fine histories of the Stolen Generations that have been written or the *Bringing Them Home* report itself. In that report, a quote from the submission by the New South Wales Link-Up organisation to the inquiry illustrates why the government's past treatment of Indigenous people has been so cataclysmically painful and damaging to them:

> We may go home, but we cannot relive our childhoods. We may reunite with our mothers, fathers, sisters, brothers, aunties, uncles, communities, but we cannot relive the 20, 30, 40 years that we spent without their love and care, and they cannot undo the grief and mourning they felt when we were separated from them. We can go home to ourselves as Aboriginals, but this does not erase the attacks inflicted on our hearts, minds, bodies and souls, by caretakers who thought their mission was to eliminate us as Aboriginals.

At no time have I ever believed that there was some kind of parallel, or in any way comparable, life experience between those of Aboriginal people separated from their families and the experiences of adoption in the wider Australian community. There were huge differences, which must be confronted and understood by us all if we are to come to terms honestly with the true history of our country. That reality is that the Stolen Generations were separated from their families because of their race, as the driving force of social policy, and that policy was directed at the first people of this land, the Aboriginal and Torres Strait Islander people of our country. The work I did in my time as minister and beyond to help bring us to confront and understand this fact was one small part of an enormous and wide-ranging effort by many, many people and organisations that is still ongoing today. I was privileged to find myself in a position as government minister where the influence I had was able to help in some small part to further this effort.

12

Meeting on the Sydney Opera House steps

Despite the setback caused by the two photographs I sent to Maida, events began to move forward to our reunion. For this, we had Sandra to thank, as she continued to wrap my mother in kindness and empathy.

On 15 January 1993, I met with Sandra at the Parramatta office of the Department of Community Services, and she gave me an update on developments. She explained Maida's state of mind following the Lansdowne Street coincidence and other revelations from the letter I had written to her in Forster. Despite her heightened fragility, I was advised that Maida had agreed to meet me.

I was overwhelmed by the prospect of finally meeting my mother, and longing for it to happen — although at the time I was also drowning in the relentless pressures of my electorate and my ministerial responsibilities as the election loomed closer. Adding to these feelings, there was now another dimension to my quest to meet with Maida as soon as possible. After learning about her suffering, I'd become convinced that I had to fulfil my obligations to her as her son. That may sound strange, but it was how I felt. She had brought me into the world; she had given me my life. I owed her my very existence, and I was determined that she must suffer no more. I had an intuitive but resolute sense of responsibility and gratitude towards her.

I knew the appalling statistics about the failure of adoption reunions, and the factors that could contribute to that. They just made me all the more determined to make this work, no matter what. Sandra had told me I could write another letter to Maida, which she would pass on. This time, along with the letter, I included some clippings and flowers from the native plants in our garden at Stanwell Park. I hoped the flowers would somehow send the message that I wanted very much for her to enter my life and become part of my world.

> *Today I heard the wonderful news that we are to meet next week. I am writing this brief note in one of Sandra's little rooms* [rooms that I knew my mother knew well] *to enclose just a few more photos, and also some flowers from the garden at Stanwell Park. I admit that I likely care more about the garden than the house we live in.*

I went on to tell my mother that I could not wait to meet her — 'how jumping over the moon and happy I am' — and I emphasised that she didn't have to be worried about anything.

If we want to cry we will cry for a while and then perhaps some more. If we want to have a quiet time for a while we will do that. Have no doubts you are doing the right thing — no doubts whatsoever!

Your idea of meeting on the Opera House steps is perfect. Sandra suggested 11 am and this is okay by me. I will keep the day free and we will be together for however long we feel appropriate. Exciting isn't it? How will we cope until then!

I would like you to pass on to Greg my very warm affection and I look forward to meeting him when you are both ready. I hope, and Jody hopes, that he will play an important role with you in the future lives of Jack and Jade, and us too of course.

Don't worry about feeling nervous about the meeting. It is perfectly understandable and I feel a little bit that way myself. But we must both have faith, and in my heart I know all will be well.

Take care until we meet.

With great love and affection,

Robert

I remember the exact spot where we embraced that first time, in that momentous and life-changing moment, on Wednesday 20 January 1993: near the corner of the far bottom step, at the left of the Opera House as you are approaching from Circular Quay. Whenever I am at the Opera House now, I never fail to go there. It became my and my mother's spot forever.

One of the reasons I remember this first meeting so clearly is because I grabbed a piece of cardboard off the back seat of my car when I arrived at the Botanic Gardens, and I made some notes as I walked along the foreshore towards the Opera House. I have kept this humble piece of cardboard for 27 years.

That first embrace with my mother Maida was a kind of coming home. I know she felt the same. She had truly waited a lifetime for this moment.

She greeted me with a simple, 'Hello, Robert,' and then we fell into each other's arms. When the embrace ended, we each took in the reality of the person in front of us. I was face to face with my beautiful mother for the very first time since I was adopted over 41 years previously.

No photograph could have adequately prepared me for meeting Maida in person. She had a high-energy personality and impressed me straight away with her spontaneity and vivaciousness. I noticed her beautiful smile and her infectious laugh, which sometimes sounded like a schoolgirl's giggle because she was so incredibly nervous. She kept saying, 'Oh, Robert! Oh, Robert!' in disbelief, while laughing and crying all at the same time.

For my part, the feelings were overwhelming, and I was so nervous that at first I could hardly speak. I kept thinking, *This can't be happening.* No other moment in my life has been so turbulent and momentous in comparison.

Neither of us said much in those first minutes; we just stood there sizing each other up. I saw that my mother was a tall, slim, and very attractive woman. Her hair was beautifully cut and permed — I suspected it was done especially for the occasion. She wore a sleeveless blue and white summer dress with a belt, and I wondered if she had agonised as long as I had about what to wear. Whether she had or not, she looked great and had made just the right choice.

After that first greeting and embrace, we had to work out what to do. There was no game plan or script for this situation, despite Sandra's work in preparing us. I suggested we could walk into the adjacent botanic gardens, and, when my mother agreed, I tentatively placed my hand on her back to guide her. I have been a shy person for most of my life, but that day I was especially nervous, and every small touch was breaking new ground.

We walked past the Opera House, mingling with the throngs of tourists and visitors, and entered the gardens from the walkway along the foreshore. Our historic meeting had a truly magnificent Sydney backdrop. On the way, we chatted about the harbour, the gardens, and the city, occasionally stopping and facing each other to prove to ourselves that this was real.

My mother thought the gardens were glorious. As we walked towards the restaurant and coffee shop, we passed a small pond with waterlilies. Here, it was quieter, and we could be alone. I saw a garden bench not far away and suggested we take a seat there. I could see that if we sat on that bench, we could face inwards towards each other, or turn front on, or even turn away from each other as necessary. It was a safe conversation space, and we needed that, because there was much to be said.

There was no guide for us, no agenda or connivance of any kind to start the process of mutual personal discovery and begin to understand what had become of our lives. It was a raw and unrehearsed meeting from beginning to end. I was too deeply involved in listening to my mother's words and responding to them to think about taking any notes. My mother, however, did have a small notepad with her to record key details to think over later, and I suspected Sandra's guiding hand.

My mother was on fire and did much of the early talking. She had waited a long time for this. I was hit with an almost incomprehensible avalanche of family history, names and places, which left me scrambling to understand how this family jigsaw fitted together. For a time, I was confused by my mother's repeated references to someone called Precious, who I assumed, at first, must be her husband, Greg. Then my mother explained to me that Precious was the latest in a long line of beloved cats, who had each occupied a prominent place in her life. But I was riveted to every word. With each sentence, I was learning more about my mother and her family. Often, she needed to stop and wipe away tears.

Occasionally she asked me to turn front on to her, so she could look into my eyes, and of course they were her eyes looking back at her. 'You have my eyes, darling Robert, and you can't escape that,' she said, laughing.

My mother mentioned names, like Adrian, Lorraine, and Brian, but it took me some time to understand that they were her siblings — and therefore, of course, my uncles and aunts. The sibling she talked most often about was her twin sister,

Cynthia (Cyn), whom she was extremely close to. Cyn had suffered from polio as a child, and had worked at The King's School (where I nearly went as a student) as a cleaner and later in hospitals doing the same work. Aunty Cyn's husband, Jack, was no longer alive, but there were two children, Jenny and Daryl (Daryl had been photographed with the same Santa as me in 1955). The whole family still had strong connections with the central-western New South Wales city of Orange. Maida's other sister, Lorraine, her husband, also called Jack, and their family still lived there, and it was clear that my mother strongly identified with Orange as her hometown, even after all these years. It was where her mother and father and grandparents (my grandparents and great-grandparents) were buried. Later, I was to learn more about the longstanding family association with Orange, and that gift of a rich family history was another valuable outcome of my adoption reunion.

That day, however, these family connections were a whole new dimension, which I hadn't considered, and I told my mother how much I looked forward to meeting my aunts and uncles and numerous cousins. At this, she again wiped away tears, and I detected some diffidence about my enthusiasm to meet the wider family. I realised this was because she had been so private and secretive for so long about her post-adoption pain. She told me that only a handful of people in the world knew that she had given birth to a child, and Cyn was the only one who understood the pain she had suffered for decades.

By far the most important person in my mother's life was her husband, Greg. Maida explained that soon after my birth she had embarked on a trip to Europe by boat — a wonderful and courageous thing to do to reclaim her life, I thought. She came from a relatively poor family, so must have undertaken some very determined saving to raise the funds. The photographs from that trip she later showed me reveal a beautiful young woman in her mid-twenties experiencing life at its best. Maida travelled with a girlfriend and stayed away for more than six months, during which time she kept substantial diaries. When I later read some of these, they revealed the depth of Greg Kirwan's feelings for her and of her friendship with him. He was to become her husband in 1957.

Maida told me Greg was a carpenter by trade and had built their house in Lansdowne Street himself in preparation for their marriage. She was proud of the fact that they'd never taken out a mortgage, but had saved to buy the modest suburban block. When Maida spoke about Greg, there was so much admiration in her voice. I immediately got the impression that she saw him as a kind of saint-like figure of wisdom and compassion, in contrast to what she perceived as her own fallibility. She explained that he had stuck by her all those years, and his steadfastness and steady hand had helped her survive. Over the rest of her life with me, she constantly described Greg as her 'rock', and gradually I came to understand what that meant. Greg was always there for her when she went to the edge, as must have happened so many times. Over time, I came to know Greg intimately, and I know that, in his later years, he saw me as the son he never had. The love and the trust between us became absolute, and continued until the day he died in 2017.

By now, we'd been talking for about two hours, and my mother was gaining the confidence to speak about some of the difficult and sensitive subjects she had never shared with any of her family or friends. It was as though she'd been saving herself for this conversation with me. I felt enormously privileged, but at the same time found it very hard, and we both sobbed at times as she tried to get her thoughts out.

My mother explained that there wasn't a single day she hadn't thought of me, but she had spoken about my birth and adoption only once to Greg, very early on in their relationship. Just one conversation in over 40 years with her soulmate. Of course, her words included outpourings of grief, and, as they came, I could hardly contain my own distress. I held her in my arms and comforted her as best I could, and both of us were grateful for the solitude and privacy we had that day in the gardens.

She then gently made it clear that she didn't want to talk about my birth and the later adoption process, which was obviously too painful for her. With a discreet aside, she made it clear that she didn't want to talk about my birth father, either. I got the very clear impression that these subjects were off limits, and I respected that.

Maida recalled the moment when the first letter from the Department of Community Services had arrived. She'd known immediately what it was about, and it was a bolt of lightning striking at the heart of her identity and existence. The letter had terrified her, and she told me how deeply distressed she had been, and that she couldn't stop crying. It had taken some time before she could tell Greg about it, even though the letter and the later call with Sandra heralded the promise of a reunion. The very thought of meeting me had compounded the sadness and the longing she had felt for so long.

The coincidental convergence around Lansdowne Street had deeply distressed her, too, but she needed to hear more to better understand what had happened, and how it could have come to be. She asked me to tell her more about 18 Lansdowne Street, Merrylands, that house of my childhood only ten doors down from her own home.

I explained that I'd often stayed at the house during the first 12 years of my life, until my grandmother had died in 1963. Most school holidays, my family would travel from Forster to visit Grandma for a time, and I'd played up and down the street, and I vividly remembered quite a few people who'd lived there. There was a Miss Ezzy, a long-term Italian resident who Maida remembered well, too, and Bernard who I remembered as 'the Dutch boy' and his family, who lived opposite my grandmother. I remembered frequenting the shop on the corner of Woodville Road, up and across from where my Aunty Daphne lived at number 6.

My mother tried to imagine me in the street as a 'cute black-haired little boy', as she described me. She told me she remembered Mr Rowley at number 6 (my Uncle Dick) and especially remembered my grandmother Mrs Osborn, who used to sit on her verandah, and who my mother passed every day on her way to and from work. We shook our heads in disbelief about these shared recollections. It was a relief to me, though, that my mother didn't remember seeing me in the street, as I'd often played out the front of my grandmother's house or sat with her on the front porch or walked on my own to visit Aunty Daphne, who used to give me little ornaments that I'd taken a liking to. It would have been just too painful for her to deal with the knowledge that the little boy she'd seen all those years ago was her own lost child.

Sandra had constantly reinforced that I should take things slowly with my mother, and although I did my best to keep this in mind, we did a lot of talking that day. Maida asked me about my own family circumstances, and, to reassure her that she hadn't caused me pain by the adoption, I spoke at great length about the happiness of my childhood. A whirlpool of conflicting emotions poured from her: gushing tears and deep distress, interspersed with her terrific spontaneous laughter. I worried about whether my protestations of the wonderful life I'd led made her relieved that I'd been well looked after or whether they caused her further pain, but eventually I understood that she felt only relief that I hadn't suffered.

She took great delight in my excitement about the birth of Jack, her grandson, which had happened only four months earlier, and had been, as I reminded her, the turning point in my decision to lift the contact veto and reach out to her. My hope was that Jack could be, in some little way, the child she'd never been able to enjoy and love; I could see, as tears poured down my mother's cheeks, that she had so much love to give. She was delighted to see more pictures of him, and I vowed to make sure that Jack would play a huge part in her life from now on. And, indeed, it was a delight as the years unfolded to see the love Jack gave Maida reciprocated in doting grandmotherly bucketfuls.

I knew it was important to give Maida confidence about the ongoing security of our relationship. At one point, I faced her, held her by the shoulders, looked into her eyes, and said, 'You need to know that now I've found you, I want you to be a special part of my family — a grandmother to Jack and Jade. And I promise you that I'm not going to go away. You're stuck with me forever, okay.' I wrapped my arms around her, and we cried again together, but I know they were tears of fulfilment and happiness.

We kept talking, and I explained the importance of growing up in Forster to my life. I told her that I'd never stopped thinking of myself as kid from the country, and she reminded me that she was one, too. I was eager to show her Forster and other key places in my life, but we were both very conscious that my mother Gwen was still living in Tuncurry in the aged-persons complex. At all times, Maida was incredibly respectful, if not deferential, towards my mother Gwen, and kept saying over and over, 'She must be such a beautiful person, Robert.'

Maida also asked me how I'd become involved in politics, and this was where our first real point of difference came out. My mother confessed that she was a lifelong Liberal Party voter. I thought this was hilarious, and we joked about our differences. Then and there, in the gardens, we made a deal that we wouldn't talk about politics again, and that remained our vow for the two decades we spent in each other's lives before Maida's death in 2012. Whenever politics came up in some way in conversation, my mother would give a little shriek and say, 'Oh, Robert!' and move on to another topic. The truth was, our different political allegiances never bothered me in the slightest. I loved Maida unconditionally, as my mother.

There was another side to Maida, too. Despite the trauma of her past, she was a strong and resilient woman, who had got on with her life and had a wonderful marriage to Greg. She told me stories that day about their travels together around different parts of Australia and overseas. The good times they'd shared over their many years together clearly filled her with joy. She had been a loyal and highly respected Parramatta City Council employee for almost 30 years, and she and Greg were debt-free, financially secure, and happy and fulfilled. I could tell, too, that they were humble people, who didn't like pretentiousness, and who had lived a very modest life during the years of their marriage. I was left with the clear impression of my mother as a strong, proud, and competent woman, who had gallantly fought the sadness of the adoption, though it had inevitably left a scar on her soul.

At the end of many hours together, I again remembered Sandra's advice that it was wise not to rush the relationship. While she hadn't said so explicitly, the implication was that Maida and I would part company in the gardens. But after what we'd just been through, it felt like it would be too artificial for words to turn my back on my mother, and for us each to make our way home alone. So, in the late afternoon, I said, 'Well, dearest mother, would you like a lift home? I already know where you live, after all,' referring, of course, to my familiarity with Lansdowne Street. She laughed and willingly accepted the lift.

As we walked through the gardens towards Mrs Macquarie's Chair, where I'd parked my car, I remembered the disposable camera in my back pocket, and asked a passing stranger to take a photograph of us.

And there we were, immortalised, with our arms around each other and with the harbour and the Opera House behind us in the distance. Mother and son, reunited.

When we arrived in Lansdowne Street, Maida invited me inside to meet Greg for the first time. As we walked from the car, I was nervous. I had no idea how Greg might feel about me. Would there be any underlying resentment about the disruption I'd caused to their lives by pursuing the adoption reunion?

I needn't have worried. Greg's manner was warm and friendly, and we shook hands enthusiastically.

'Thank you so much for being a part of this,' I said. 'I know it's a bit overwhelming, but I know things will settle down and everything will turn out fine.'

He replied in a strong, calming voice, 'I'm sure it will.'

I was conscious that it had been a long day for my mother, so I gave her one last hug, gave Greg a big wave, said goodbye, and left. As I jumped into the car, I saw that Maida and Greg had come outside to farewell me, which had the instant effect of making me feel part of the family.

I headed up Lansdowne Street and stopped in front of number 18. I imagined myself as that little black-haired boy sitting on the verandah with my grandmother, and felt a wave of gratitude and privilege sweep over me.

Driving back to Stanwell Park, I felt uplifted and empowered, but, at the same time, I desperately wanted to know more about how my mother was feeling. I still wasn't even close to fully understanding that.

13

Learning my birth father's name

As the new year progressed, I felt daunted as I contemplated how I was going to deal with the ongoing emotion of this adoption reunion while also maintaining some privacy, continuing my work as a local member serving my electorate in a marginal seat, and managing my public life as the federal minister for Aboriginal and Torres Strait Islander affairs at a time of huge public debate around the Australian government's response to the Mabo decision. (Readers who want to know more about the turbulent politics of the time can read my book *Taking a Stand*, which deals with these and related issues in great detail.)

The Mabo decision in 1992 was recognised as one of the most important decisions of the High Court. It overturned what was called 'the doctrine of terra nullius' (land belonging to no one), and it recognised, for the first time in the history of our country, the concept of native title in those places where Aboriginal and Torres Strait Islander people were able to prove their continuing connection with the land, and where the land had not otherwise been legally transferred to the control of others, as in the case of freehold land. The challenge for the government was how to respond to this decision. One option was to leave it to hundreds of separate court cases to determine the existence of native title in specific cases. Alternatively, we could set up a specialist tribunal to determine if native title existed in such cases. The specialist tribunal was ultimately the chosen course.

The government was also determined to protect the rights of Indigenous people that were newly recognised by the court, and to advance the rights of those Indigenous people who would not fall within the High Court decision. The battle lines were drawn, with the opposition led by conservative state governments (including some ALP governments) and the mining and pastoral industries, which were backed by allies in the Liberal and National parties in Canberra. This turmoil had already erupted by early January, as I was preparing for my reunion meeting with Maida.

By contrast, my first two-and-a-half years in the portfolio had been a period of cross-party cooperation and a time of sweeping reform in Aboriginal and Torres Strait Islander Affairs policy. As a backbench member, I had always worked hard to try to bring out the best in people and to work in a cross-party way wherever I could. I took this approach in my work chairing the Parliamentary Group of Amnesty International, and in chairing the Joint Standing Committee of Public Accounts where all the reports were unanimously adopted by members from all political parties. With this history and way of working, I was able to secure unanimous parliamentary support for legislation to initiate and formalise the process of reconciliation between Aboriginal and Torres Strait Islander communities and the wider Australian community. The intention was to make this reconciliation process one of the core objectives of the nation as we moved towards the celebration of the centenary year in 2001, and indeed so it became. It was a landmark achievement for the parliament and for the country.

The newly established Aboriginal and Torres Strait Islander Commission was allowed to progress its important work, and both the shadow minister for Aboriginal and Torres Strait Islander affairs, Michael Wooldridge (later health minister in the Howard government), and the opposition leader, John Hewson, worked cooperatively with me and the government to set up the Council for Aboriginal Reconciliation. People from all walks of life responded to my invitation to join the council, including some of the key opinion leaders in the Aboriginal and Torres Strait Islander community. Thanks to the efforts of Bob Hawke, Patrick Dodson accepted the invitation to chair the council. Sir Ronald Wilson became the deputy chair, and, following his death, Ian Viner, a former Fraser-government minister, took on that role. Even those who were usually seen as the warriors for the Indigenous cause but who weren't on the council were won over to give the work of the council a chance. They were inspired that Pat Dodson had taken on the role of chair.

The legislation to create the council set a three-fold agenda. Firstly, the council was to use the period in the lead-up to the centenary of Federation to educate the wider Australian community about Aboriginal and Torres Strait Islander history and culture. This included teaching the history of dispossession, which I'd always believed was fundamental to the country coming to terms honestly with its own history. From my own school history text-book, I had seen how desperately it was needed. Secondly, there was a high-level expression of intent in the legislation that the Commonwealth would seek an ongoing national commitment from governments at all levels to cooperate and to coordinate with the Aboriginal and Torres Strait Islander Commission towards certain goals. These goals were to address Aboriginal disadvantage and aspirations in relation to land, housing, law and justice, cultural heritage, education, employment, health, infrastructure, economic development, and any other relevant matters in the decade leading to the centenary. Finally, the legislation made it clear that one of the potential outcomes of the process was a document of reconciliation, but the council was to keep open the potential final name or description of that document. (This was to overcome the historic resistance of the Coalition to the use of the word 'treaty'.)

By January 1993, when I reunited with Maida, my strategy was beginning to unravel because of events beyond my control. The mining and pastoral industries, some state premiers, and conservative broadcasters began to attack not only the Mabo decision, but, on occasion, the High Court itself. My intention in the lead-up to the election scheduled in early 1993 was to keep a lid on the more acrimonious debates about the Mabo decision, as I knew the public interest would not be served by the Coalition declaring war on Indigenous affairs. The Mabo debate, as it was euphemistically called, generated massive ongoing newspaper headlines, and was often the lead item on the nightly TV news. As minister for Aboriginal and Torres Strait Islander affairs, I was right at the heart of this combat zone, leaving precious little time to reflect on or take the important next steps in my and Maida's adoption reunion, or even just to spend more time with Maida, as I wished to do. I was also very worried about the potential for my privacy to be invaded — or, even more importantly, for Maida's privacy to be put at risk. The idea of some tabloid newspaper photographing my mother standing at her front gate in Merrylands and adding some salacious headline filled me with terror.

Out of necessity, I limited the people I could confide in and seek solace and guidance from. On one occasion I did, however, choose to confide in someone I'd only just met, and it turned out to be a decision that would lead to yet another striking coincidence coming into play.

In my work fighting for Aboriginal and Torres Strait Islander rights, I met with many diverse groups in the Australian community, including the leaders of the various churches and faiths. I found that, almost without exception, these leaders were strong supporters of the process of reconciliation, and also fully onside in the campaign to secure strong Australian government legislation to respond to the Mabo decision. Not long after my first reunion with Maida, I was invited to attend a dinner at a weekend retreat organised by the Australian Catholic Bishops Conference. I spoke to the bishops warmly and openly, and, as was my usual practice with such groups, took them into my confidence about the challenges that lay ahead. I felt very welcome at the event and very trusting that my briefing would be respected.

After the dinner, I ended up falling into easy conversation with the highly respected Bishop William (Bill) Brennan, a leading Catholic social-justice advocate, who had spent a good chunk of his life working closely with Aboriginal people in western New South Wales. He had a warm and friendly manner, which inspired trust, and during our chat I felt the need to share with him my story about meeting my birth mother. Our reunion was ever-present in my mind at that time. Bill listened intently and was clearly deeply moved by my account of my meeting with Maida and what I told him of her life circumstances. I then told him about the incredible coincidence of Lansdowne Street: how my mother had lived only ten houses away from my adopted grandmother, whose house had been my second home during my childhood. When I mentioned Maida's address, his mouth dropped open and he slumped back in his chair.

'I've met your mother,' he said. 'My sister lives just a few houses away in Lansdowne Street, and they know each other well.'

I asked him not to say anything to anyone, and he touched my hand in an act of reassurance and comfort. He readily understood just how fragile my mother was and that she had never told anyone in the street that she had given birth to a child so many years ago.

I left the gathering soon afterwards and drove back to Stanwell Park, marvelling at the amazing way my political life and my personal life had just intersected.

Within a week of our first meeting, Maida and Greg drove to Stanwell Park for the first time and met Jack, Jade, and Jody. The house we lived in was modest, but set back and down from the road and surrounded by a prolific garden, most of which I had lovingly planted. We were all ready for their arrival and had prepared a lunch on the back deck among the tree tops.

When they came to the door, we were there waiting, me holding Jack. Maida reached out and took him in her arms and nursed him for much of the time she was there. Her bountiful joy was a sight to behold; she was clearly drinking up every moment, and she treated Jack as precious cargo. I could see that Greg was very pleased to be there, too, and was taking it all in, in his own quiet way. The old phrase 'still waters run deep' was so true of Greg, and it was clear that he saw the deep significance of this event for my mother.

Maida and Greg fitted into our household easily, and over time they came to meet a wider circle of our friends and acquaintances in the neighbourhood. At first, Maida was very nervous about meeting anyone, but gradually she became comfortable about being introduced as my mother. She was a regular visitor to Stanwell Park, often driving down from Merrylands on her own while I was away in Canberra and other places. Sometimes, we went for family walks in the nearby Royal National Park, with me carrying Jack on my back. Maida and Greg had become part of the family, as I'd promised they would.

On election night — 13 March 1993 — my personal and political life came face to face in a very public way. I was returned as the member for Hughes, and my mother was photographed with the rest of our family at the victory celebration in my electorate office. The photograph appeared prominently in the *St George and Sutherland Shire Leader*, a major regional newspaper. Although Maida wasn't identified by name, she was very recognisable in the photograph to anyone who knew her. I don't think she'd realised that the photograph was likely to appear in a newspaper, and I should have warned her. Unfortunately, I hadn't realised that things were still very precarious for her and didn't fully appreciate her fragility.

Following the election, I invited Maida to Canberra for the opening of the new parliament, and she agreed to come, but during the visit she was clearly torn with conflicting emotions. While she was proud of me and pleased to be with me and my family, she was also still petrified of coming out as my mother. My staff did their best to make her feel comfortable and welcome in my ministerial office and also at the opening events, including the official reception, held on the occasion of the opening of parliament. Di Hudson, in particular, was very kind to Maida and did her best to look after her, but it was all overwhelming for my mother — and who could blame her? In a little over three months she had come from 40-plus years of secrecy and sadness to attending an official reception with her newly reunited son in the new Parliament House in Canberra — an event where she was formally introduced to the prime minister, Paul Keating, and the governor-general of Australia, Bill Hayden. It was simply all too much.

My mother fled to a private place, where I found her sobbing in the corner. I felt so bad. My intentions had been good — I'd wanted to share my public life with her — but I'd forgotten her extreme vulnerability and had expected too much. We took greater steps to look after her for her remaining time in Canberra, and I realised that I had to be a better son.

By now, my mother's family knew about her deep, dark secret and were becoming impatient to meet me. All roads seemed to lead to Orange, and I decided I needed to go there with Maida as soon as possible. But the first step was to meet my Aunty Cyn, Maida's twin.

My first meeting with Aunty Cyn is etched in my memory. I arrived with my mother at Cyn's house in Wentworthville in western Sydney. It was a modest house, like Maida's, and also like Maida's, it held a lot of love. Cyn's little bent frame rushed towards me, and she gave me a wholehearted hug and kiss. It was such a warm and effusive greeting I was almost bowled over.

'Welcome back to the family,' she said enthusiastically as she hugged me again and kissed me as if she'd known me all her life.

'Great to be here,' I said.

She retorted with, 'What took you so long?'

I couldn't help but think how lucky Maida had been to dodge this terrible polio bullet. By a wicked throw of the dice, Cyn had contracted polio as a young girl, and as a result had missed out on critical schooling. She'd worked as a cleaner for most of her life, which must have been excruciatingly painful and difficult for her at times, as she was severely bent over due to the polio. Later, she had lost her husband in tragic circumstances, far too early. Despite these events, Cyn had still lived a good life, as evidenced by all the family photographs around the house.

She was so moved by my arrival back into my mother's life that she looked at me with deferential awe, as if in the presence of a miracle. While I was embarrassed by this attention and played it down, I understood that she was just so pleased to see Maida experience this joy in her later life. Aunty Cyn was so deeply aware of my mother's suffering that it had become etched into her own life and persona. As twin sisters, they had shared each other's pain, and Aunty Cyn had been on that journey with my mother every step of the way.

My cousins, Cyn's daughter, Jenny, and her son, Daryl (from the Santa photograph), were there to meet me, too. As to be expected of cousins born of twins, we have some similar features and are all tall and dark-haired. Daryl has a very caring nature and has worked as a dedicated hospital support person for most of his life, while Jenny has been a nurse in both general and psychiatric hospitals, and has spent time living in the UK. She has a great sense of humour, and I partly recognised myself in her uninhibited and quirky eagerness to engage with people.

We were now ready for the trip to Orange. My mother and I headed off one wintry day in late May of 1993. I met her brother Brian, who lived in Wellington, and his wife, Yvonne, and two cousins, Robert and Charlie. I also met her older sister, Lorraine, who lived in Orange with her husband, Jack. Lorraine and Jack had three children, who, like me, were eager to meet a new cousin. I felt immediately at ease with Gary, Julie, and Helen, and all my new-found family. They'd pre-empted this meeting by sending a card welcoming me to the family, with Helen adding a note that with my presence 'the family is complete'. I was very touched.

Jack and Lorraine hosted a family dinner that night, and as we all sat around their dining room, the surreal nature of the gathering caught up with me. I just couldn't believe that I'd gone from having no biological family members to being surrounded by a room full of them. And all were happy to welcome me to the family as a long-lost nephew or cousin.

Maida took me to see the house in Byng Street where she'd grown up, opposite which radio broadcaster John Laws had at some point lived, so the family confided to me. She also took great pride in showing me her childhood school, as well as where she'd worked in the town before leaving for Sydney to have me. My mother was very proud of her family's long association with Orange, as now am I.

After our trip to Orange, the next big step was to take Maida to Forster so she could better understand the life I had lived without her during those critical formative years. It was a trip we both wanted to happen, but it would not be easy. I was torn, because I deeply wanted to share my childhood memories with her, but I knew this was likely to be extremely painful, as she would be reminded of how much she had missed. I was also worried about how Maida would cope with the realisation that my mother Gwen and her could possibly finally meet. This would bring together the two women who had so shaped my life. Maida obliquely alluded to these challenges before we left, and I could sense from her clipped and truncated conversation that there was some tension in the air.

Nevertheless, we set off, just the two of us, late one Friday in May of 1993. Driving through the night, my head was spinning with crazy thoughts. I just knew that at some stage during the four-hour drive, the conversation would turn to the question of my birth father. I had determinedly avoided the slightest hint at the subject since first meeting my mother several months ago, partly because Sandra had educated me well on the sensitivities of this issue, but also because by now I had a deeper understanding of my mother's vulnerability. The truth is, asking about my father hadn't been a priority for me; my focus at that time was very much on Maida's wellbeing. But that's not the same as saying that I was uninterested in who my father could be or whether he was still alive.

I thought that around Newcastle might be the time to tentatively broach the subject in some oblique and general way, without in any way alarming my mother. But as it turned out, I didn't have to ask. My mother initiated the critical conversation herself, saying out of the blue, 'Would you like to know anything about your birth father?'

Both the content of her question and the sudden way she said it made me think that this was something she'd been considering for a while.

'Look, my focus is on you, and my absolute loyalty is with you, and it can be no other way. That's the way I want it,' I said, and kept driving.

We were silent for a time, and then Maida said, 'But you deserve to know, don't you?'

I just kept focusing on the road in front of me. The silence between us was unnerving, but I was determined not to push it until she was ready.

'I want to tell you,' she said, 'but there are two conditions.'

'Of course, whatever you want,' I said immediately. And I meant it. I desperately wanted to know his name, but it had to be on my mother's terms.

'Firstly, I don't want you to contact him until I'm ready for it. And secondly, I don't want you to speak of me or reveal anything about me.'

'Of course,' I said again.

'His name is Leonard Douglass Murray,' she said. 'The spelling of his second name is unusual …' She muttered something so softly I could barely hear it over the noise of the road — something about a 'double s' in his second name. I realised that she was implying that perhaps that would make it easier to find him.

'Okay, thanks,' I said, not wanting to sound too excited. In fact, I was so grateful and fired up that my grip on the steering wheel had become vice-like. I was so particularly moved that Maida was telling me the name of my birth father, because it was obviously such a huge act of selfless love. She had a deep integrity, which meant that she recognised that I had a right to know, and she wouldn't stand in the way of that.

Maida told me one final detail: my birth father had grown up in the Sutherland Shire. This, of course, intrigued me, because half my electorate of Hughes was based in the Sutherland Shire. Still, I remained calm, with my eyes focused on the road ahead. I felt that any show of excitement or overt interest might be seen as disloyalty or betrayal so soon after our beautiful reunion. Maida had every right to be in charge of this process; I fully respected this without question. I was immensely impressed by the strength of character she'd shown in setting some ground rules for contact right from the outset in order to protect herself.

The rest of our trip to Forster was uneventful by comparison, but it meant a lot to me to be able to show my mother the house where I'd lived with Mum and Dad, where I'd gone to school, the pool where I'd swum, the beaches where I'd surfed, and all my other memories from the town.

During the two days we were in Forster-Tuncurry, we stayed in my mother Gwen's unit, which had not yet been sold. Our presence in the unit raised another difficult ethical question. I still had it in the back of my mind that it would be wonderful if mother Maida could meet mother Gwen. Mum was still living in the aged-persons complex a couple of blocks — only 300 metres — away, and was still able to recognise me and have meaningful conversations, but her memory and capacity were fading fast due to the impact of the dementia. I couldn't help suggesting to Maida the possibility of introducing her to mother Gwen while there was still the chance that Mum could appreciate what was happening. Maida was adamant that it wasn't the right thing to do, and I dropped the suggestion immediately. I went to see my mother Gwen on my own, while Maida remained at the unit.

14

Giving in to temptation

There was no question of me not following my mother's wishes about seeking a reunion with my birth father — I'd promised to wait until she was ready for that step. But naturally my curiosity was deeply aroused from the moment I heard his name. As it turned out, it was well over a year before Maida indicated that she was ready for me to attempt a potential reunion. For me, that wait was difficult.

Then again, there was no barrier to me trying to find out more about him in the interim, and I wasted no time in doing so. The day after that illuminating trip to Forster with my mother, I was in Darwin to fulfil a ministerial commitment. Free for a moment that afternoon, I went to the Commonwealth electoral office to look up the electoral rolls for New South Wales, which were still public at that time. I managed to find a Leonard Douglass Murray on the electoral roll at Mangrove Mountain, inland from Gosford in New South Wales, and suddenly had a flashback to that one-off conversation my mother Gwen had had with me when I was a little boy. She had mentioned the name Beasley (Maida's family name) and had also said something about my father being an electrical engineer or something similar. I remembered exactly where we were in the house in Lake Street when we had had that talk, so it must have been significant for me at the time. *Was* my father an electrical engineer, or had I confused something in my child's mind?

When I looked again at the roll, I saw four other Murrays at the same address: Craig, Jeanette, Lola, and Neil. I assumed that one of the female names was my father's wife, and it suddenly hit me that the others might be my siblings. I was truly dumbstruck. Of course, I should have considered the possibility of having brothers and sisters before this, but I hadn't. Just meeting my birth father had seemed a crazy outside possibility, given all that I'd read about the unlikelihood of successful meetings between adopted children and their birth fathers. But now there was the possibility of at least three potential siblings, maybe more.

I am ashamed to confess that later that night in my Darwin hotel room, I did something irresponsible. Thankfully no one was hurt in the process. Through directory assistance, I got a phone number for the address at Mangrove Mountain. I had no intention of having a conversation with my birth father, but I thought it could do no harm to simply hear his voice if he answered.

I called the number.

When the call was answered — by a man, perhaps my father — I had a rush of blood to the head and spontaneously asked for a 'Mr Jackson', the first name that came into my head.

By weird coincidence, the man replied that a Mr Jackson had once lived at that address, but was no longer there.

We exchanged a few words before I sheepishly and quickly ended the call. I immediately regretted what I'd done, and of course I had no idea if I had just spoken to my father, or even whether he was still alive.

When I returned to Sydney, I made use of the snippet of information I'd received from my mother about my father growing up in the Sutherland Shire. I went to the State Library of New South Wales in Macquarie Street to search the electoral rolls for the period when I estimated he'd lived there. Bingo! I quickly found Leonard Douglass Murray and his father (my grandfather, who was listed as a railway worker) at an address in Gymea Bay Road, Gymea. Coincidentally, this road was at one time the border between my electorate of Hughes and the neighbouring electorate of Cook. Later that day, I drove there and found that the old house was still standing, with two giant old palms out the front.

But I was still a long way from any possible family reunion with my father — and perhaps my siblings, too. The months marched on without any indication from Maida that she was ready for me to take the next step. I became very anxious about it all, and developed a morbid fear that my father might die before I met him. After all, I had no idea about the state of his health.

I put my mind to work to see if there was any more information I could find and suddenly remembered one of my very close friends in the Sutherland Shire, Hazel Wilson. Hazel had lived in the area a long time, and had stood against me for preselection as federal member for Hughes in 1984. When she was eliminated from the ballot, it was her preferences that helped get me elected.

I called Hazel, and after a little chat about local politics, asked her if she'd ever come across a Leonard Murray while growing up in the Shire. I didn't explain why I was asking, just waited for her response, pressing my hand into the desk in anticipation. I suspected that she was a similar age to my father, which she later proved to be.

I was dumbfounded when she replied, 'Yes, I grew up with him. I knew him well.'

'I don't suppose you have a photo of him?' I asked, almost jumping out of my skin at the thought.

'Doubt it, but I'll have a look.'

I was grateful that she didn't ask me why I was enquiring about him. Much later, she told me that she knew I was adopted and therefore had her vague suspicions. I was astounded by how perceptive she'd been.

A week went by, and I still hadn't heard from Hazel, so I phoned again to remind her. A few days later, she dropped a tiny envelope in to my office.

I opened it eagerly to find an even smaller photograph inside. It was old and discoloured and showed a group of young people in, of all places, Stanwell Park in 1947. My father would have been only 20 years old at the time. He was standing behind two other young people, a man and a woman, who were seated, and he was posing with his hands

170

on their shoulders. In yet another extraordinary coincidence, the woman whose shoulder my father was touching was Hazel Wilson. I couldn't believe my luck that the one person I'd asked about my father not only knew him well, but had a photograph of them together.

Even though I couldn't see his face clearly, even with a magnifying glass, he looked reasonably tall and well built. I was excited beyond belief. The photograph made me feel closer to him, despite the fact that I could not make out his facial features.

My next detective foray some months later brought me dangerously close to being caught out and, worse still, inadvertently violating my mother's wishes.

I'd decided to drive to Mangrove Mountain to see where my father lived. I had no intention of making contact of any kind, but just felt I wanted to be near him. When I found the address, it seemed to be a modest-sized farm, and the house wasn't visible from the road. I felt stupid sitting in my old Nissan Skyline opposite the farm gate, imagining what the house beyond the rise might look like and wondering whether my father was in there, only a couple of hundred metres away. My heart was pounding, and my nerves were raw.

I had a scheduled radio interview with John Doyle on 2BL that afternoon, and did it on my mobile phone (which was the size of a house brick in those days) while still sitting in the car I'd inherited from my father Bert out the front of my father Len's house on a remote road in Mangrove Mountain.

It was all pretty weird, and I fantasised about how amazing it would be if my father happened to be listening to the interview inside the house.

Then, just as the interview finished, I got a terrible shock. A car slowly came down the driveway to the front gate. A woman got out, opened the gate, and started to walk over to me.

'Are you okay?' she called. 'Can I help?'

Panicked, I jumped out of the car and mumbled something incomprehensible about tyre trouble, trying to turn my face away as I spoke. I told the woman I was fine, quickly returned to my car, and fled. She must have thought I was some weird stalker, which would have been a reasonable conclusion in the circumstances. Later, once I'd regained my composure, I realised she must have been my father's wife, and that made me feel even worse.

As I drove home, chastened and ashamed, I thought about how selfish I had been. Who was I to intrude into this family? What if my father didn't want to meet me? What if he didn't even know I existed? Or was so ashamed of me that he'd never told his wife and the rest of his family? I could have been responsible for destroying a family.

I was a mess.

I was also consumed by an all-powerful urge to meet my birth father. Somehow, I was convinced that it was all meant to be, and that, ultimately, we would meet.

15

Grieving for Mother Gwen

My responsibilities as a local MP took on a new dimension in January 1994 when catastrophic bushfires ravaged the Royal National Park that I loved so much, destroying 90 per cent of it and leaving a charred, blackened moonscape. And things were to get even worse. On the afternoon of 8 January, the fires escaped the bushland around the Woronora River in the Sutherland Shire and burned through the adjacent suburbs of Como, Jannali, and Bonnet Bay. It was a terror-stricken time for the residents, as the fire took over the streets. Dozens of homes were destroyed, and a woman lost her life.

The community response in the aftermath of the fire was inspirational. People rallied together to help. My electorate-office team were part of that, and responded to hundreds of requests for assistance.

On the evening of 13 January, as I was on the way to a major public meeting that had been called in the aftermath of the fires, I got a call on my mobile phone from my old family friend Doctor Sanders in Forster. My heart was in my mouth, as I could think of few reasons why Doctor Sanders would be calling me, and I feared the worst.

'I have some bad news, I'm afraid,' he told me. 'Your mum has just passed away. There was nothing we could do for her.'

'Did she suffer?' I asked. 'Were you there? Can you tell me about it, please? I need to know?'

The thought of my precious mother dying all alone sickened me. I felt immediate guilt that I hadn't been with her.

'I was there, and she was very much at peace,' he reassured me.

I was grief-stricken and in shock. My beloved mother, who had given me so much, and who I was closer to than anyone else in the world, was gone. Although she had been deteriorating mentally, she had otherwise seemed to be in robust good health, and her death hit me hard. I was bereft and sobbed inconsolably in my car, parked on the Princes Highway at Engadine. I phoned Jody, and she consoled me as best she could, but I was so distressed I didn't know if I could drive the car. I sat by the roadside for a time to let it all sink in.

Just as when my father had died, I was torn between my private grief and my public responsibilities. As the local federal MP, I was expected to attend this important community meeting, where I knew people would also be grieving for their losses. Tensions would be high, and there was a strong expectation that I would assist the community with information about rebuilding, insurance, and social-security-related issues.

I drove to the meeting and did what I could, and told no one what had just happened.

Mum's funeral was held in Forster a week later, at the local Uniting Church just across the road from where I lived as a child. Mum's friends and family came to the service, and Maida drove up from Sydney, too, to pay her own special tribute to the venerated person who had taken on the role of bringing up her son.

Afterwards, I returned to work immediately, not taking any time to process my mother's death. I deeply regret this, as the loss and grief hit me like a ton of bricks two years later in 1996, after I lost my seat in the election of that year. These days, I'm the first to tell people that grieving is such an important thing to do when you lose someone precious.

After my mother Gwen's death, my yearning to meet my birth father increased. I kept my pledge to Maida not to make contact, but fervently hoped that she would raise the topic again soon.

I knew that approaching my father directly would have been ethically wrong for other reasons, too. There were established processes for making the initial contact, which Sandra at the Department of Community Services would undoubtedly manage when the time came. Any transgression of these processes was fraught with danger.

At this stage, though, it was all academic. Without Maida being comfortable with me proceeding, my hope to meet my father wasn't going anywhere.

When liberty was granted some months later, it came without warning. I was drinking coffee with Maida in her kitchen when she quietly said, 'Look, Robert, I'm okay with it now, if you want to follow up.'

I looked at her, not yet clear on what I was being told.

She added, 'You know, with the other party to all this.'

I smiled, and caressed her arm to reassure her. 'Whatever happens, if anything, you can be assured that nothing will change with us in any way. You're my mother forever, and my commitment is to you absolutely.'

'Please don't forget what I told you about the way I want this handled,' she reminded me, but I didn't need reminding. Being an intensely private person, she didn't want my father or his family to know anything about her. It was a very reasonable request.

'Of course,' I told her. 'I'll honour your wishes, there's no doubt about that.'

No matter how much I tried to smother my feelings, she could see that I was deeply grateful to her. Once again, it was a powerful testament to the strength of my mother's character that she managed this process so magnificently. I had read about many reunions with relinquishing mothers that had been unwittingly damaged by children rushing to meet their birth fathers. Maida was having none of that, and I respected her so much for her wisdom and strength.

16

An exchange of letters

I got in touch with Sandra and told her I was now ready to see if contact with my father could be made. In her kind way, Sandra later telephoned Maida to check that she was coping with this recent development, as indeed she was.

Sandra swung into action and made first contact, in the form of a discreet letter from the department asking my father to get in touch about an event 'a long time in the past'. The letter didn't elicit a response.

Some weeks later, Sandra sent another similar letter, but again there was no response. Of course, at the time, I wondered if the lack of response was a sign of rejection.

Despite this setback, I was unshakeable in my belief that the reunion would occur, and I pleaded with Sandra not to give up. 'I know it will happen,' I kept telling her. After all that had happened, I just couldn't conceive of failure as an option.

Sandra had to explain to me that we were getting to the

point where further communication would be inappropriate and outside departmental guidelines. She made it clear that such letters could constitute harassment, and we may have reached the end of the road.

I pleaded with her to give it one more go. 'Just one more try. I know it'll work.'

I guess my buoyant optimism and determination were persuasive, because Sandra did give it just one more try. A week or so later, she called me to say that she'd been successful. She'd called the Mangrove Mountain house, and my father had picked up the phone. The conversation was open, warm, and engaging, and he was very much interested in making contact with me.

I was in the Northern Territory at the time to finalise the handing back of some Aboriginal land to its traditional owners. I was ecstatic to receive the news, but of course I couldn't share it with the people I was travelling with. Instead, my joy found its expression in my particularly excited and upbeat mood that day.

Sandra followed up by writing to my father on 4 July 1994, and she also enclosed a letter from me. I later retrieved her letter from my father and cringed to read the following assurance from Sandra given the context, unknown to Sandra, of my early inadvertent stalking incident:

> I would again like to take this opportunity of reinforcing that you have nothing to fear regarding contact with Robert. He is a person with respect for privacy and is aware of the issues his contact with you may hold for you and/or family.

Be assured therefore that you need not fear unannounced visits and the like.

My father's handwriting, when I eventually saw it, was very elegant. My own dreadful script in the letter forwarded with Sandra's must have made him severely doubt that we could be related. Once again, I forwent a salutation:

This is probably one of the most unusual letters you will ever receive but I hope one of the most important ones. Please excuse my poor writing. I could have typed this letter, but even though my handwriting is terrible it is more personal to write than to type.

I hope with all my heart that you will welcome my letter and understand how much I want to meet you. You need to know that this person who is your son poses no threat to you and your way of life. I am fully aware how sensitive and difficult my existence may be for you and possibly to other members of your family. You need to know from me right from the beginning that I try to be a caring and sensitive person, and in the period ahead will try to give effect to those principles.

You also need to know right from the beginning that my wish to meet and establish a possible relationship with you is totally separate from any person you knew in your past life. I have no interest whatsoever in talking about the past. But I am a human being and you are my father and I want to meet you so very much.

I believe that you may have had other children and I hope

in time I may be able to meet them too. I have no other brothers or sisters.

The good news is that I am modestly very confident that you will like me. Just for the record I am tall, reasonably well built, have dark hair and a very friendly personality. [In hindsight I cringe at the things I wrote.]

I have had a most wonderful life. I grew up in a town on the North Coast of NSW (Forster) and was always very comfortable with the fact that I was adopted. My adopted mother and father gave me a great life and every opportunity that a person could wish for. My adopted father was in a range of successful small businesses and gave a lot to people in the community through his voluntary efforts teaching children to swim. My mother died only two months ago. She was wonderful.

I am married and have two children, Jade and Jack. My wife Jody and I have been married for nearly 8 years and I became the instant father of Jade, who was then six years old. Baby Jack is now 18 months old and was the first person in the world who actually looked like me, however he has blond hair and mine is dark. He is of course your grandson and he is wonderful!

I have worked very hard in my life and have been fortunate enough to be successful in what I have done. I was able to go to university and have a couple of law degrees and an economics degree. But I am not working as a lawyer. I have to warn you that my job has made me somewhat of a public figure in the community. I hope that when you do find out my name, you will form your own judgments about me, not from what you read or see but from meeting me and knowing me. I am modestly proud of what I have done in my life and what I stand for, however the public me is not the real me!

I have deliberately not contacted you directly because I recognise the sensitive nature of the issues and the need to proceed cautiously. For this reason I have approached Sandra of the Family Reunion section of the Adoptions Branch of the State Department of Community Services. I know Sandra to be a very caring person and I am confident that she will be very sensitive in making contact with you.

I should tell you about an incredible coincidence. I know very little about your past life but was told the general area where you grew up — Gymea. I immediately thought of a trusted personal friend in the area who would be about your age and asked her if she knew your name, without telling her why I wanted to know. My friend told me she knew you when she was growing up. I asked her if she had a photograph of you, and she found one of a big group of people taken at Stanwell Park, which is the town where I now live. The coincidence is even more remarkable because in this big group of people you have your hand on my friend's shoulder and that of another young girl. [In fact, the other person whose shoulder my father was touching was a young man.] *However the photograph doesn't help me much because it is so tiny that your face isn't clear even with the use of a magnifying glass. But what an unbelievable coincidence!*

To write to you takes a bit of courage on my part. It may well take a bit of courage on your part to take a step into the

*unknown to meet me. But don't worry, all will be well. After
all, I am your son.*

*I would like to conclude my letter by stressing that I am
a very down to earth person. I am very 'together' in my life
and have no hang-ups of any kind about the circumstances
of my birth and my adoption.*

*I know this must be a big development in your life. It is
certainly a big development in my life, and probably like
you I am of course a bit nervous about it all. However I feel
confident that it will work out for the best, and I hope you
feel the same.*

Respectfully yours and warmest of personal regards,
Robert

I didn't know when I wrote this letter about a
fundamental problem facing a possible reunion with my
father. I subsequently learnt from Sandra that my father
had never mentioned to his devoted wife, Lola, nor to my
brothers and sisters, who then ranged in age from 24 to
33, that he had fathered a child in his mid-twenties. In
many families, this may be less of an issue, but in the case
of my father, there was a risk it would affect his family's
perceptions of his character and personality. My father and
Lola had been married for over 30 years, and they were
both of a strong Christian faith and very caring and loving
people. My father was seen by the family as someone of
outstanding integrity: a devoted husband and father, who
had lived a very thoughtful and ethical life. But, despite
this, he had kept an enormous and morally complicated

secret from the people he loved the most in the world. Understandably, he was concerned about how they would react to the shock of that revelation.

Sandra told me that my father was determined to sort out these things before we met. I just had to wait for him to share the shocking news with his family and, after all that had happened, to determine when he was ready to meet me — if indeed he was still prepared to do so. The wait was excruciating, and I started to worry more and more about any hurt to others my arrival on the scene might be causing.

To this day, I have no knowledge of what happened behind the scenes when my father told Lola and my brothers and sisters about my existence, nor of what their first reactions were. I guess I don't want to know. But it would have been very natural if there were tears and deep shock. I suspect there must have been some hurt and even anger directed towards me, too; they would be less than human if this was not the case. Despite our closeness now, that has, of course, always been their private business with my father, and I have always respected that.

In the interim, my father replied to my scribbly note with a beautiful handwritten letter. It was warm and friendly, and contained a photograph taken at Port Arthur in Tasmania some years previously. He looked very different from the blur in the old picture of him with Hazel, although his features were still not completely clear in this new photograph.

My father let me know how pleased he was that I'd grown up in happy circumstances and had had a satisfying life. He went on to say,

… the strangest coincidence is that I have always thought of
you — at least in earlier years — as 'Wee Robbie' without
really knowing your name. I still have a vision of you, having
nursed you as a babe at the hospital where you were born,
looking more advanced than you were at the time. My sister
Dulcie, then a nurse, was with me at the time. So you can
understand then in no small measure that not only are you a
human being as you say, but a very special one, and my son.

I felt very connected to him reading these heartfelt words
and the emotion within them. But I was shocked to read that
my father had held me as a baby in the hospital. I had never
been told this by my mother.

I was intrigued and surprised by what I read next:

… the assurances made to me after you were born about
your prospects for the future were well founded. Forgive me
for talking about the past in this way, but I do not think
I should dwell on it as you have rightly said.

My father's letter made clear that he looked forward
to meeting me soon, and went on to talk about Lola's
reaction:

… although Lola knew nothing about us until a week ago
she has been magnificent in her attitude and I value her
understanding and support as it is an important phase in
our lives. She is also most involved and is looking forward
to meeting with you all. I am a lucky man.

He continued:

I should tell you a little of myself. Born at Marrickville, where we lived with my grandmother for five years, and then to Chatswood where I went to school for five years, thence to Gymea where we had a poultry farm. My mother worked hard at undertaking what my father could not do until he retired at 65 from the railway. I milked a cow, fed chooks before leaving for school, and used a single furrowed plough for growing green feed and vegetables. I used to transport 30 dozen eggs on the handlebars of my bike to the shop at Gymea Bay owned by Les Johnson. [This was the same Les Johnson who was my predecessor as local member in the federal seat of Hughes.]

I served an electrical apprenticeship with the Sutherland Shire Council [a stone's throw from my electorate office in Sutherland] *and these skills enabled me to become the youngest electrical installation inspector in NSW when I got to Orange.*

So, there was *a connection with electricity,* I thought, remembering what my mother Gwen had told me all those years ago as a small boy.

My father said that in Orange he had lived in the single man's flat at the fire station, and that he had been very involved in many community-based organisations in the town. Given my own background before politics, I was intrigued to read that he had begun legal studies as a young man, but was forced to suspend them when he moved overseas to take a job running the Honiara power supply in the Solomon Islands. He had taken up these studies again in his retirement. Without having any idea yet what I did for a living, my father also recounted that his New Zealand cousins had told him that 'our ancestors for about 600 years have been farmers, doctors and lawyers as well as politicians'. I was delighted to see that I was mentioned twice in these categorisations.

He mentioned that despite being a non-smoker, asthma and chronic airways disease had caused him to retire from his later work in the insurance business. My own lungs had never been strong, and I wondered what my future might hold in this regard. I decided to try to get back to regular swimming when I could.

I was especially excited when I saw that my father had revealed the first substantive information about my siblings, Jeanette, Kathryn, Neil, and Craig, and something about their family circumstances.

Finally, I was pleased to read his reassurance that he wouldn't be deterred by any public image I might have:

> You should rest assured, Robert, that I would not make judgements of you, public image or otherwise. I am confident (a gut feeling if you like) that you will be a representation of your grandfather Archie (Archibald) who was admired and respected by all who knew him, diligent and sincere.
>
> I am pleased with all the thoughts that you expressed in your letter and I relate to them all and pray that all will move steadily and directly to that focal point of unity and happiness continuing.

Any adopted person getting a letter like this from their birth father would have to feel they'd won the lottery, and indeed I did.

My next letter to my father contained more personal information about myself, my family, and my job, to be passed on by Sandra when she believed the time was right. I also enclosed some photographs that showed various snippets of my life, mostly of a family nature:

> *Your letter was just wonderful. I don't think I could have wished for more. The fact that you held me as a baby is just extraordinary and so special.*

I thought it very important to reach out to Lola, too, and to express my deep appreciation for her support for the reunion process. She could have responded so very differently, but clearly had thought things through deeply and had come to a point of acceptance and resolution. I am sure this was helped by the fact that her sister had adopted children, which meant the issues were not unknown to her.

> *I would like to say to Lola how much I appreciate her warmth and understanding and that I will never let her down in my friendship. I am confident that she too will enjoy what lies ahead. But for now, good on her for being so supportive!*

Much later, Lola told me, tongue in cheek, and with a laugh, that if the events of my birth had occurred during the 30 years or so she and my father were together, things might have been very different. I found her wisdom and graciousness to be another uplifting aspect of the adoption reunion process.

I expressed my delight at finding out I had brothers and sisters, and let my father know what a big deal this was for me:

> *I never thought that would happen to me. They seem a fine bunch, but I guess it will take a while to work it all through. But for them too, I am no threat.*

I hoped that one day my siblings might get to read this letter and my positive message of reassurance.

My father replied to my letter two weeks later, again through Sandra. This correspondence was very much a trust-building process, expertly managed by Sandra, to move step by step towards a reunion, and hopefully to build strong foundations for a future relationship.

My father had been very moved by my letter and confided that it was 'all overwhelming' for him. He also acknowledged my heartfelt feelings directed to Lola and confirmed that her support meant a great deal to him. 'I do not know how I would fare otherwise,' he confessed.

Now knowing my identity and my ministerial role, he made an astonishing admission:

... in one of my earlier letters, Lola had suggested that we omit to mention Craig's chosen career in the police service, because if you were on the 'other side of the tracks' it could cause problems.

I thought this was a fantastic revelation, and showed that they had wanted to progress the reunion even if I were a well-known criminal! I also learnt that my father and Lola had been engaged in their own version of stalking to try to find out who with a public profile lived in Stanwell Park, which was the only detail they had about me at that time. They hadn't managed to work it out, and of course there was no internet for them to access in those years.

I had already discovered that my father grew up knowing Les Johnson, my predecessor in the seat of Hughes, but my father now mentioned that just prior to our contact, he'd been in the Sutherland Shire and spent some time with Les. My father had been visiting the Shire to attend the funeral of a well-known local identity (whom I also knew well). The funeral had been held only a few blocks from my electorate office.

In this letter, my father also mentioned that he hadn't yet told my siblings of my existence. I sensed some trepidation in him about the challenges this might involve. He and Lola wanted to speak to each of my brothers and sisters face to face, but they wanted to tell my sister Kath first, as she was living away from the rest of the family in Brisbane. They were scheduled to visit her in November, which was some four months away. I was a little worried that such a long delay in telling them might compound the shock, but of course I didn't consider offering a view on such matters. I could only hope that everything would be handled with great compassion and sensitivity — and I expected it would be from all that I had read from my father so far.

I received one further letter from my father in July. Sandra faxed it to my office in Canberra while I was overseas at a meeting of the UN Working Group on Indigenous Populations, which was in the course of preparing a draft declaration on Indigenous rights. In the letter, my father said that Lola had seen the photographs I'd sent with my letter and had been 'amazed at your likeness to Neil at his graduation in photographs she had just received from him'. In a later letter, after I arrived back from overseas, he mentioned an approaching family 'special occasion' to celebrate Neil's engagement to his future wife, Nereda. Craig, Jeanette, and Kath were also excited about the event, and my father wrote, 'It always has been a close, caring family and hopefully it will continue of "pentagonal" proportions in the foreseeable future.'

I was deeply touched that he considered me to be the final side of the pentagon, but it was a daunting prospect, too. Depending on the response of my siblings, I might not be welcomed into the family as we hoped.

17

Meeting my birth father, brothers, and sisters

A week after this letter, in August 1994, I received the momentous news from Sandra that my father was ready to meet with me.

When I'd met my mother for the first time, we'd chosen a Sydney landmark as our meeting place, so I thought it fitting to choose another landmark place to meet my father. I proposed the Pyrmont Bridge, as I had a long history with it. I was one of the campaigners against its proposed demolition when I was a city councillor back in the early 1980s. Opened in 1902, the bridge is a Sydney icon of sorts, linking the business district with the adjacent suburb of Pyrmont. It passes over Cockle Bay, a small horseshoe-shaped bay that is now part of the Darling Harbour entertainment area. A pedestrian and cycle bridge these days, it was once used by motor traffic and had a swing span that would rotate to allow boat traffic to pass.

My father and I were to meet in the middle of the bridge, which is predominantly made from Australian ironbark timber, tough as nails and designed to survive. I thought this a good omen for our reunion.

I got up early on the day of our meeting, fired up and ready to go. It was a picture-perfect late winter's day without a cloud in the sky as I drove from Stanwell Park to the city. Even so, after parking the car, I began to grow increasingly anxious as I walked towards the bridge. Although I'd seen photographs of my father, they weren't detailed enough to give me a strong sense of what he looked like. As it had been with Maida, I seriously worried that I might not recognise him. I hadn't spoken to him yet, either, apart from my mystery call to his house in the months after my mother had first given me his name 18 months previously — and even then, I hadn't been sure it was him I'd spoken to. I scanned my surrounds as I walked along, worrying that he might even be walking beside me without my having realised.

When I reached the agreed spot in the centre of the bridge, I couldn't see any sign of him, and the frightening thought hit me that he might have changed his mind.

I waited for what seemed like an eternity, but was probably only a few minutes, and then I saw a man in the distance who seemed to be looking for someone. He saw me, and we both smiled tentatively as we began to approach one another from about 50 metres away.

We kept walking towards each other through the heavy pedestrian traffic on the bridge, and the smiles got bigger the closer we got. On meeting, we spontaneously wrapped our arms around each other in a loving embrace and held it for some time. I don't think I have ever met anyone in my life with whom I felt so completely and immediately at home.

'Hello, my father,' I said, my arms still around him, gazing into his eyes for what was to me the first time.

He, of course, had looked into my eyes in Crown Street Hospital all those years ago, but he was now nearly 67 years old, so it had been a long time between hugs. He was clearly just as awed by this moment as I was. He smiled and said, 'Hello, my son, what a wonderful day in our lives.' He had a soft and gentle voice, which quavered with emotion, and that drew me to him even more.

He had dressed up for the occasion, as I should have expected from his letters, in a light fawn suit and a tie with diagonal red stripes. He wasn't quite as tall as I'd expected, but he looked fit and in good health.

We hadn't thought where to go after this initial meeting, so I suggested coffee at one of the restaurants on the western side of Darling Harbour. In truth, I didn't really care where we went; it was just so wonderful to finally meet my father.

At first we were hesitant in our conversation, but our confidence grew as we felt increasingly comfortable in each other's company, and soon virtually nothing was off limits. This was when I thought it timely to remind him of something important.

'I just want to mention one little thing, if that's okay?'

'Of course,' he said.

'My mother has requested that I don't talk about her in any way, and I have to respect that.' I didn't use Maida's name, as even that seemed like a breach of faith in my mind.

'I understand,' he said, and that was that.

I was relieved, as I'd been struggling with how I was going to deal with this elephant in the room. I didn't want to intrude into the personal feelings of either my mother or my father, or into the circumstances of their relationship all those years ago in Orange. From the beginning, I thought it was none of my business. It was ancient history and didn't impact on my life in any way — except for, of course, that I was the outcome of that relationship. That was all I needed to know. I had been given the gift of two new families, and that was enough for me.

We had so many questions to ask each other as we sat for hours in that cafe. Occasionally we pinched each other to confirm that we really were there, together. There was so much I wanted to know about: my grandparents; his health; growing up in the Sutherland Shire; his life story; how he was living life now; and so on. He wanted to know about my life, too, of course, and I shared everything with him except the taboo subject of my earlier reunion with my mother.

There were two subjects where I waited for him to take the lead. One was about his wife, Lola. I felt so deeply grateful for the forgiveness and understanding she had shown to my father, and for her unwavering support for this reunion. It could not have happened without her, and I was forever in her debt. I wanted my father to tell me about her and their life together, but only when he was ready. When he did speak of her, it was to describe a very fulfilling and happy marriage, and I could see his love and respect for her in his eyes.

The other subject was that of my sisters and brothers. I was already walking on eggshells here, and started to worry when, after several hours, my father still hadn't mentioned them. Perhaps something had gone wrong.

When he did eventually speak about them, he admitted, 'Your arrival on the scene has been a huge shock to them.'

I immediately felt wretched, and experienced another rush of guilt about my selfishness in pursuing this reunion.

Then he added, 'I think the shock was as much or more about me than you,' and I understood more fully the implications of what must have been a huge guilty secret in his life.

Yet another of the many coincidences surrounding my adoption came to light when my father mentioned the address of the former family home in Gordon where my siblings had grown up. I realised that, over the years, while taking a regular short cut on my way to Forster, I had frequently driven right past that house.

After we'd talked for several hours and the sun had moved over the proverbial yardarm, I suggested we have a glass of wine. My father, being a loving and sensitive man, happily agreed, not telling me that he wasn't a drinker, or that Lola, a definite teetotaller, was in fact waiting to meet us on the other side of the bridge. I still shudder to think what she must have thought about me that day when she smelt the wine on my father's breath. Perhaps that I'd dragged him into bad company on day one!

It was only as we were walking back across Pyrmont Bridge that my father mentioned that Lola would be waiting for us in front of the Sydney Aquarium. I think he must have forgotten this while we were talking, overawed by the magnitude of events. Or maybe he did tell me that she was waiting for us, and I didn't hear it because of my own emotions. In any event, I would have stopped talking hours before had I realised Lola had been waiting so patiently for us.

As we walked towards my first meeting with Lola, my mind was going crazy. I felt totally unprepared. How should I handle it? Should I be cautious, or show my enthusiasm with a hug?

Lola was standing on the wharf just in front of the aquarium, watching us walk towards her. She had a welcoming smile on her face, and I decided to just be myself. I gave her a warm hug, which was immediately reciprocated. I was overjoyed to be so welcomed.

I don't remember the details of what we said to each other, because our meeting was such a shock to me, but I do remember that we chatted easily, and I thanked her profusely for her support for the reunion with my father. She said she was looking forward to meeting Jody, Jade, and Jack.

After we'd promised to see each other again soon, I stood waving goodbye until my father and Lola disappeared from sight. I felt dazed, as if in a trance. Could all that have really just happened?

I walked aimlessly for a time, ending up on the other side of Cockle Bay, looking up at the place on the bridge where we'd just met. It had been such a big day for me, and it couldn't have gone better. I'd experienced a deep feeling of fulfilment and connectedness to my father, and saw in so many small and large ways how he had been the missing element in my life. This first meeting had given me huge insights into my own self and what I perceived to be some of my defining qualities, especially my gut-response empathy when I'm confronted by human suffering.

I was still concerned, though, that there might be unresolved issues with my siblings, and I didn't really know the details of where my father was up to in telling them the full story about me. I was tremendously excited by the thought of having brothers and sisters, but equally apprehensive and fearful of rejection.

Soon after this first meeting with my father, he phoned to tell me that he'd now told the full detailed story of my birth all those years ago to each of my siblings, and it was likely that meetings would be set up soon. It all happened very quickly after that.

The first meeting was at the house of my sister Jeanette, the oldest of my siblings at 33 years old, in Ryde. I was to meet Jeanette and her husband, Sel, and her daughter, my niece, Alana (nine months younger than Jack). Also present was my father's sister, Aunty Dulcie. My father and Lola were there, too, of course.

As I walked up the drive towards the front door, I steadied myself for what was to come: meeting my sister and aunt for the first time was another big moment in the family reunion process. I needn't have worried. Everyone was there at the front door to greet me, all as excited as I was.

Unknown to Jeanette, I'd first heard of her and her daughter, Alana, almost two years previously, during one of my furtive visits to Mangrove Mountain. I'd called in at the one-pump service station and picked up a copy of *The Mangrove Mountain and District News*, a small local paper. In it, I'd seen an item about Len and Lola Murray announcing the birth of their first grandchild, Alana, born in Melbourne to Jeanette and Sel. I took great delight in recounting this story to Jeanette, and also revealing my guilty secret about driving up to where my father lived.

She laughed, clearly liking the story.

Wow! This warm, vivacious, larger-than-life person is my sister, I thought. Right from the start I was elated and proud to be her sibling. At that time, Jeanette was a nurse in the spinal unit at Royal North Shore Hospital. Since then, she has moved into the inner city, closer to where I live, and now works in community health, including delivering programs supporting the Aboriginal community in the inner west of Sydney.

My Aunty Dulcie was two years younger than my father, tall, slim, and well dressed. Meeting her was particularly special, because I'd learnt from my father Len that she had actually held me as a baby in Crown Street Hospital in my first week of life. When we met again, she gazed at me as if I were a revered species (much to my embarrassment), and I felt humbled by her kindness.

She spoke in a quiet but direct way, and greeted me by holding both my hands in hers. 'Welcome to the family,' she said.

'I've heard that you held me as a baby,' I said. I still found this so hard to believe.

'Yes, and a beautiful baby you were, too.'

'Amazing — and good to see you again,' I joked, and she gave me a little grin.

Aunty Dulcie was a very kind and loving woman, who had devoted her life to her Christian faith and her missionary work in rural Australia. She lived a very modest and frugal life until the day she died in 2015. Although we were very different and I didn't share her faith, we became very close. I admired the integrity with which she had lived her life, holding true to her beliefs and convictions. I visited her regularly over the next two decades, and joined the rest of the family in spending time with her in the week before she died, at peace with herself and with her God.

My brother Neil cut through the reunion process by directly phoning my ministerial office in Canberra. I was in Adelaide when I got the message that he'd phoned, and called him back immediately with my heart in my mouth, somewhat petrified that it might not be a friendly call. I could barely talk I was so nervous, but as soon as I heard his warm, strong, and confident voice, I knew everything would be okay.

Neil is the older of my two brothers, both of whom are younger than my sisters, and he was then 28. We agreed to catch up as soon as I got back to Sydney, near where he worked at the time as property manager for the Sydney Cove Authority. He has since gone on to have an extremely successful career in property management in both the public and private sectors, and is highly regarded in the industry.

We met one weeknight after work, and it was just like it had been meeting my father. As I walked into the venue, this bloke stood up from his chair and strode over to meet me. It immediately hit me that we did indeed share quite a strong resemblance, as Lola had said. We were of virtually identical height and build, and had similar facial features.

We greeted each other with a tentative handshake, and a degree of trepidation on my part. I so wanted this to work. We sat down and had our first drink together, and the conversation flowed. We just fitted like a glove, and I discovered for the very first time in my life what it might be like to have a brother.

At one point as we were chatting happily, I looked down at his hands on the table in front of me, and it was just like looking at my own hands. I could hardly believe it.

'Those are my hands!' I blurted out, and he laughed at my delight in such a simple but wonderful thing.

My brother Craig was next to appear on the scene. He was 24 years old and a police officer in Sydney. Craig first made contact with me by letter, which began with a confronting statement, before continuing reassuringly:

Just over 24 hours ago Dad told me the news, and yes, I have been on a roller-coaster of emotions. I love our father so very

My mother Gwen's favourite baby photo, which also became a favourite of Maida's

My adoring mother with her new baby, soon after taking me home to Forster

All dressed up to attend a family wedding

Just south of Rockhampton on the long road to Cairns — a holiday in our Sunliner caravan

Surfing Pebbly, my favourite beach

Me (far right) with Meredith Burgmann being arrested at the golf during
an anti-apartheid protest against Gary Player (not pictured)

Mother Gwen and Grandma Minnie on the porch at 18 Lansdowne Street, Merrylands

Mother Maida sitting on the step at 38 Lansdowne Street, Merrylands, where she and Greg had lived since their marriage in 1957, just ten doors down from my grandmother

Me with Santa in 1955 in Parramatta

My cousin Daryl (son of my mother's twin sister) with the same Santa the same year. My mother Maida was present when this photo was taken.

Looking down from the Opera House steps while I wait for my first meeting with my mother. She is a speck in the distance.

Me and my mother Maida that same day. Photograph taken by a passing stranger

The first photo I ever saw of my mother Maida, taken in Ash Street, Sydney

My mother Maida as a young woman in Orange in 1951, the year I was born

My mother Maida in Italy in 1954

Mother Maida taking her grandson, Jack, into her arms from his sister, Jade

With mother Maida and Greg at 38 Lansdowne Street, Merrylands

My father Len (circled) standing behind my friend Hazel Wilson.
The photo was taken at Stanwell Park in 1947.

First meeting with my father Len, on Pyrmont Bridge, Sydney

With my two brothers, Neil (middle) and Craig (right),
and my father Len on the occasion of Neil's wedding.

My four siblings (from left to right) — Craig, Jeanette, Neil, and
Kath — and me, with my father Len and Lola

much. He is a wonderful man who would do anything for anyone. He has always been there for me and I have always been there for him. Rob, there is so much to write about, I can't possibly fit it all in this letter, not if I wrote all day and night. Dad has explained everything and I asked a lot of questions. You have not been out of my mind. Last night when I was driving back to Sydney from Mangrove Mountain, only about 2 km from our front gate tears welled in my eyes. I felt a mixture of emotions. Well, now it is Wednesday and all is well. I don't know why I felt like I did and it must be a natural process.

Craig told me that my work as minister for Aboriginal and Torres Strait Islander affairs was known to him, and that, when he was at the Police Academy, he had quoted me in an essay and a class presentation. I was quite chuffed and amused that he had done so not knowing that I was his brother.

He closed his letter with some very warm words about welcoming me to the family. Not long after, we arranged to meet at the same place where I'd met Neil. I got there first, because I wanted to be able to see Craig arrive; I'd learnt through experience that I found it easier that way.

I saw him as soon as he came through the door. He was tall and well built, with lighter-coloured hair than Neil and different features — more like our father's. He was so enthusiastic and animated about everything he spoke of. He struck me as someone who was just itching to throw himself into life and experience everything around him.

Craig shared with me his longstanding involvement in public speaking and his interest in studying law, which, of course, were huge parallels with my own interests and background. He's now a solicitor, running his own busy law practice in Sydney.

He also has a deep and resonant speaking voice, and when I commented on it, he responded by imitating the Australian TV journalist Peter Harvey, who was known for his distinctive sign-off at the end of his reports. 'Craig Murray, Canberra,' Craig declaimed in his deepest voice, and we both had a good laugh.

We immediately formed a strong bond and had some warm and funny experiences getting to know each other. Not so long after this first meeting, we went on a car trip to visit his grandmother on his mother's side at Alstonville, near Ballina. I drove, and we discovered during the trip that we shared a very old-fashioned, and some would argue poor, taste in music. Craig had brought some John Denver along, and was flabbergasted when I turned on my music in my car and it was also John Denver.

We stayed overnight in Forster at my mother Gwen's unit, which I still had. That night, we reverted to ridiculous adolescent brotherly mischief. After dinner at a local restaurant, we competed in a running race through the streets of Tuncurry back to the unit, and then ended up wrestling on the floor. Naturally, Craig's 24-year-old body and massive frame put my 44-year-old body to the test. It was as if we were making up for the time we'd missed out on growing up together.

I had another memorable experience with Craig, which reinforced my new role as part of a large and loving family. He invited me for a catch-up on Sydney's Lower North Shore, and noticed when I returned from getting a drink that I was very quiet and obviously distressed. He asked me what was wrong, but at first I refused to tell him. Eventually he dragged it out of me that I'd been harangued about my political views by a very pompous and aggressive voter. I hated confrontations of this kind and always shied away from them.

With lightning speed, my 24-year-old brother jumped to his feet and headed in the direction of my antagonist. I was mortified, but there was nothing I could do to stop him. There he was, towering over my heckler, talking vigorously, and gesticulating for emphasis. I was quite anxious, as the situation could have easily gotten out of hand, but Craig finished making his point and returned to our table. And it suddenly hit me that, now I'd become part of this loyal and supportive family, I would never be alone again. I was truly touched — more than Craig will ever know.

My sister Kathryn was a dedicated teacher by profession and was still living in Brisbane, so we were the last to meet. Kath has always been her own person, and it took some time for us to become close, not helped by a few hiccups unrelated to us directly. The turning point came on Christmas Day in 2001, when the whole family was gathered in the park at the back of my house in Balmain. During the afternoon, unknown to any of us, my father's hip replacement became dislodged, and the excruciating pain caused him to collapse unconscious. An ambulance was called, and, within minutes, the rest of us were left standing in the park as the paramedics took my father and Lola to the emergency department. At that point, we had no idea what had happened and were worried that he might have suffered a stroke or a heart attack.

There is no doubt in my mind that this scary moment helped to bring Kathryn and me closer together. We both realised how short and precious life is, and we organised a meeting for just the two of us and began the process of building our own relationship. It was worth the wait.

Not long after, Kathryn invited me to her house for dinner. I almost died of embarrassment when we opened the take-away food I'd purchased and we found it was riddled with maggots. It's a good thing we both have a sense of humour. We laughed about the irony of it all and never looked back from there.

I am as devoted to Kathryn as I am to my other siblings, and was especially proud when she became a volunteer in the refugee support programs we ran at Australian Red Cross when I was CEO.

My sisters and brothers have never treated me as a half-brother, and I certainly don't think of myself that way in relation to them. From almost the very beginning, they made me feel like an integral part of the family. Within weeks of our first meeting, for example, Neil invited me to be a groomsman at his wedding to Nereda. I was overwhelmed by this invitation and what it showed of Neil's courage and generosity of spirit.

I sometimes joke that I cheated by coming into the family as an adult. I got to enjoy and benefit from my siblings' love, friendship, and company, without any of the memories of childhood fights or rivalries. Of course, my tongue is firmly planted in my cheek when I say this, because I wish I had known them all my life. To have the love of a brother or a sister, let alone four of them, is just fantastic. My life has been transformed and enriched as a result of knowing them. I know they are there for me until the day I die, as I am for them.

There were four of them before I arrived, and now we are five. A pentagon indeed.

18

Big life changes

All these uplifting personal developments were overlaid by the relentless stresses of my political life, which only got worse after the 1993 election. After the ALP's win, the attacks on the Mabo decision and the government's response intensified, and they continued until the 1996 election. During my time as federal member for Hughes and later as a minister, I experienced the joys of a dead rat in the mail, a serious arson attack on my office, death threats, the presence of guards out the front of my home, and a disgruntled family-law litigant, who distributed an aggressive letter in the street where I lived.

Finally, I had to deal with highly political attacks on my work and reputation through the Hindmarsh Island heritage application, which continued from 1994, past the end of my career in politics, and through to the year 2000, when I was ultimately vindicated by a decision of the Federal Court of Australia. Entire substantive books have been written about the complexity of the so-called 'Hindmarsh Island Affair', including the independently written epic tome *The Meeting of the Waters* by Margaret Simons, who was Malcolm Fraser's biographer. I agree with virtually everything in that book, even though I was not consulted in its writing. The issues were exceedingly complex, but they began with a heritage protection application under Commonwealth legislation. This application was made to me by a group of Ngarrindjeri women who were opposing the construction of a bridge from Goolwa to Hindmarsh Island near the mouth of the Murray River. The site, which would be destroyed by the construction of the bridge, was of great significance to them, but their beliefs surrounding that significance were confidential.

As I was required to do by law, I commissioned an independent report, which was prepared by eminent Australian lawyer Professor Cheryl Saunders. Among other things, the report found that the confidential women's beliefs were honestly held by the women and that the issue was of supreme cultural and spiritual significance to the Ngarrindjeri women. I issued the declaration for heritage protection in line with the recommendation and report. My decision was upheld by votes in the House of Representatives, with both the Democrats and the Greens voting with the government.

Being the minister for Aboriginal and Torres Strait Islander affairs is no regular job, and I had found it increasingly difficult to balance my massive political responsibilities with my family life. Being away so much for prolonged periods, returning home riddled with stress, then spending the weekends undertaking electorate commitments was not a good formula for an enduring marriage. Jody had been heroic throughout our marriage, taking on the role of representing me in the electorate while I was in Canberra or travelling around Australia with my Aboriginal and Torres Strait Islander Affairs portfolio, but our relationship couldn't survive the huge strain of my political life. We separated in late 1994 just as the Hindmarsh Island saga was unfolding.

Then, two days after my marriage had collapsed and I was barely able to function as a human being, I was asked a tag-team series of questions in the parliament as a prelude to calls for my resignation by the opposition. It was falsely suggested in the parliament that I had been careless in my handling of confidential documents related to the Hindmarsh Island court case, but it was quickly revealed within the hour that this was not the case. In fact, an opposition front-bench member, Ian McLachlan, had secretly sanctioned the opening and photocopying of a large box of documents from the Australian government solicitor intended for my office. The box was then resealed and was later received by my office, which did not know that it had been violated. Mr McLachlan was later forced to resign, and opposition leader John Howard was under serious pressure for his role in this saga.

Next, my decision to grant the declaration for heritage protection was successfully challenged in the courts. And then, out of the blue, came allegations in the media that the claims relating to the sacred site had been fabricated. The state Liberal government in South Australia, in a political move to attack me, called a Royal Commission, which the Ngarrindjeri women seeking heritage protection refused to recognise. Even though the Royal Commission did not even take evidence from the women, it found that there had been a fabrication. Professor Saunders and I and others were then sued by the developers who were seeking to build the bridge to their property development, and this court case went on for the next seven years, long after I ceased to be a member of parliament.

Both the Ngarrindjeri women claiming heritage protection and those of us sued by the developers were ultimately vindicated by the decision of the Federal Court of Australia, which, for the first time in all the investigations, heard evidence from all parties. In my case, this involved six days of cross-examination, and it was clearly established that I had followed Commonwealth legal advice every step of the way and had acted in good faith. The attempts by the developers to gain compensation were rejected, and no appeal proceeded. The case has gone down in Australian political folklore as a cause célèbre, in which I was ultimately absolutely vindicated — but the personal toll was immense, as you can well imagine.

After Jody and I separated, I initially slept on my electorate-office floor, and then rented a shed — a very basic converted garage, with a mattress on the floor and a plastic table and chairs — in the backyard of a family living in Stanwell Park. I rented it so I could stay close to Jade and Jack. Jade is still my daughter of course, and we remain close to this day. Though it was a horrible time in my life, I have very precious memories of three-year-old Jack sharing the mattress with me when he visited on weekends. I was living in this shed when the 1996 election was called.

I spent election day, 2 March 1996, as I always did — touring the polling booths in my electorate and thanking ALP branch members and supporters for their help in the campaign. I knew it was going to be a tough election, and the polls were looking dreadful. I could only hope that my 12 years' hard work as a local member would help me survive.

My Murray family came out in strength for me, staffing polling booths in the western part of my electorate in Menai and Liverpool, and their loyal presence made me feel very proud. But despite their helpful efforts, and those of hundreds of stalwart supporters, the swing against me and against the ALP government was too substantial. My seat and many others were lost.

I was in my electorate office in Sutherland, with Maida, Jody, and Jack, when the news came through. I did a live cross to one of the TV networks, conceding defeat and thanking my supporters, many of whom were very distressed. Thankfully, I managed to hold it together as the situation required of me.

When a political life is over in such a manner, it's a brutal process. On the Monday morning after the election, my ministerial staff in Canberra, led by Di Hudson, began the job of clearing out the office. In only a matter of a few short days, my life's public work was reduced to a huge volume of cardboard boxes. The boxes were sent from Canberra and Sutherland to Maida and Greg's home in Merrylands, where they remained in a garden shed for the next 20 years.

I retreated to a shed, too — the one in Stanwell Park. I felt lost and demoralised, as did my staff. For years, none of us could drive past our former electorate office in Sutherland without feeling a sense of rejection, betrayal, and shame that non-political people would find difficult to understand. We had given everything we had to the local community for 12 years and felt trashed when they voted us out.

On 22 April, standing in a long queue in the city and waiting to exchange my diplomatic passport for a regular one, I realised that I had no job, no marriage, and not the slightest idea what to do with myself. For some reason, at that moment I remembered a photograph I'd recently seen of a sculpture park near Broken Hill in western New South Wales. The park was the outcome of an international sculpture symposium convened by an old acquaintance of mine, Lawrence Beck. Suddenly, I made the decision to drive out to Broken Hill to see it. I abandoned the passport queue, collected my car from the car park, and immediately headed west.

During my short time in Broken Hill, Anzac Day was celebrated. I watched the Anzac service, standing somewhat mournfully on my own at the back of the crowd — a world away from the high-profile political life I had been living less than two months earlier. Then, after the service, I went out to the remote hillside to look at the sculptures I'd heard so much about. The sculptures themselves were wonderful, but perhaps even more striking was the outback behind them, stretching out to the horizon. I was captivated, and I decided to keep on driving. After a night's rest, I left Broken Hill behind and headed west into South Australia. I was on the road and free to roam.

I'd left Sydney with no spare clothes whatsoever, and I was still driving my father Bert's Nissan Skyline. The car was already quite old and had done a lot of kilometres, and I wasn't sure how far it would take me. But I didn't care. In some ways, this was a bolt for freedom: to have time on my own in a way I'd never had before. I had seen most of Australia many times over, but this trip was different. I was doing it on my terms, free of immediate work or study commitments for the first time since I was a small child. Although I felt a bit lost at first, the lure of the road soon drew me in.

I bought a tent and some clothes at a store in Port Augusta, then continued on my journey until I'd driven all around Australia. I camped most of the time, but treated myself to a motel when I wanted to. And I made two trips back to Sydney to see Jack and Jade, and to fulfil speaking engagements I was committed to. For most of the time, I was alone, and I engaged in periods of deep reflection as I embarked on this pilgrimage around our wide brown land. Looking back, I think this beautiful but sometimes isolated period of reflection helped me to grow as a person.

The aftermath of my election defeat was one of the most difficult periods of my life. I went from being a government minister to being unemployed overnight. And, despite my desperate efforts to get a job, that unemployment became long term.

It was a very challenging time for me in other respects, too. I was the subject of an ongoing attack by the new prime minister, John Howard, who rejoiced very publicly in my high-profile defeat whenever the opportunity presented itself — whether at Liberal Party events or on talkback radio. I bear him no resentment for this; it was just politics. But it did make it difficult for me to get a senior role in the not-for-profit sector at that time. My efforts were further stymied by what I perceived as an ongoing vendetta against me by a well-known Sydney talkback-radio presenter, after he'd personally launched the election campaign of my opponent in the seat of Hughes. It's very hard to get work when a high-rating radio personality is ripping you apart on a regular basis.

It was also during this time that I finally learnt that you cannot hide from grief. The death of my mother Gwen, the election defeat, the end of my marriage, and a sustained period of unemployment all combined in late 1996 to knock me down as though I'd been run over by a bus.

My grief was compounded by the election of Pauline Hanson as the independent member for Ipswich and her attacks on Indigenous-affairs policy, as well as the failure of Prime Minister John Howard to issue an apology to the Stolen Generations, and his government's concerted attempt to undermine the advances I had secured for Aboriginal and Torres Strait Islander people during my time as minister. I was particularly distressed to see my work in promoting a just reconciliation for our country being torn asunder. Pauline Hanson had been expelled from the Liberal Party during the 1996 election because of a letter that she'd written to *The Queensland Times*, in which she'd attacked me over my comments concerning the hugely disproportionate rate of Indigenous incarceration. Nevertheless, following the election of the Coalition government, Indigenous programs were being slashed and reforms were reversed.

I felt quite desperate as my period of unemployment extended into its second year. I wrote 70 substantive job applications and provided a swag of highly respected referees, but still I couldn't get a job. I became very depressed, as most people who are unemployed do, but was too embarrassed to seek professional help. Despite my professional experience, I despaired of finding work, especially when many in the not-for-profit sector admitted that employing me would risk their relationship with the new Coalition government. I was a captive of my former incarnation as a politician, and no one wanted to know me as a prospective employee.

My friendship with Tom Uren and Christine Logan was one of the key things that got me through this period. I had no fixed place of abode as I had gotten myself into a terrible financial predicament with a high level of outstanding debts incurred in the misjudged confident expectation that I would get a job. I alternated between housesitting for friends and staying in the flat at the back of Tom and Christine's house. Tom's fatherly advice that 'there is no progress in hate' — that those who allow bitterness and recriminations to dominate their lives will be consumed by them — was another valuable life lesson.

In this very difficult time, my birth families on both my mother's and father's side also sustained me. They provided the love and kindness that pulled me through.

My relationship with Maida and Greg continued to develop beautifully, and I called them and saw them regularly over the years ahead. After my marriage to Jody collapsed, they were a great support to me. At this age, Jade was increasingly independent, but I saw Jack once a fortnight, and would inevitably take him to visit Maida and Greg then. They, in turn, continued to visit Jody, Jade, and Jack in Stanwell Park. Greg was a devoted grandad, or 'Poppy' as he was called, and built Jack a go-cart with his skilled carpenter's hands.

My relationship with my mother blossomed and strengthened each year, and I made sure to spoil her and celebrate her on her birthday, Christmas Day, Mother's Day, and perhaps most of all on my Christmas Eve birthday, which was such a sensitive date for her. I had a lot to catch up on, and I wanted to constantly reinforce that our reunion was permanent. We remained extremely close.

After two years of unemployment, I was finally able to get a part-time role on a tribunal using my legal background. For the next two years, I travelled New South Wales, taking any work on the tribunal I could get.

Then came the breakthrough of being chosen to be CEO of a national not-for-profit employment network called Job Futures. For this, I owe a debt of gratitude to the chair of the board, Andy Small, former CEO of the Zurich Insurance Group in Australia. I was well suited to this role, and could draw on my management skills, as well as my knowledge and contacts, to transform the organisation and increase its capacity. Most important to my value in this role, however, was my own experience of a prolonged period of unemployment. I had grown enormously as a human being during that time, and I was able to employ those life lessons to lead an organisation that helped to get long-term unemployed jobseekers, former offenders, people with disabilities, asylum seekers, Aboriginal jobseekers, and non-English-speaking jobseekers into meaningful employment. I loved the work, and I very much valued being back in the full-time workforce myself, working alongside exceptional people, whose values I shared.

After five years leading Job Futures, I was appointed CEO of Australian Red Cross, where I spent ten years working with some inspirational volunteers and staff within the organisation. The chair of the board who appointed me was Greg Vickery, ironically, a former president of the Australian Young Liberals. Greg had devoted much of his life to Red Cross as a volunteer, and, like me, he left his politics at the door upon joining Red Cross.

Greg gave me the management responsibility of transforming Red Cross from a noble but old-world organisation with eight state and territory boards and eight CEOs into a cohesive, efficient national body. The reformed Red Cross operates with one national board with governance authority, and has a sharper priority focus on people experiencing high-level vulnerability, including Aboriginal and Torres Strait Islander people. These were reforms that the organisation had struggled to implement since before

World War II. They were achieved by winning the hearts and minds of the people in the organisation and gaining their unanimous support for the changes. I was privileged beyond measure to be a part of all this, and then to twice take on the role of Acting Under Secretary General of the International Federation of Red Cross and Red Crescent Societies, based in Geneva.

Like most of us must, I have had to reinvent myself as I've moved through life. I hope to continue to do so, while always maintaining some continuing core values.

19

Nature or nurture?

My reflections on my adoption family reunion wouldn't be complete without some elaboration of the rich family history I inherited through my birth parents, some of which was relevant to my political life as well as my personal life.

My Murray family on my grandfather's side had New Zealand and Scottish connections, but it was my grandmother, Margaret Murray (nee Douglass), who provided the links with colonial Australia. I was astounded to learn that my great-great-great-great-great-grandfather James Lewis (aka Duce) was speared to death by Aboriginal people on Pelican Island — now called Dowadee Island, adjacent to Soldiers Point within Port Stephens, New South Wales — towards the end of April 1824. Port Stephens is also the local extremity of the territory of the Worimi people, the traditional owners of the area around Forster where I grew up. This seemed to me to be a superb irony, given my ministerial portfolio and my public championing of the process of reconciliation with the first people of this land.

I also discovered that James Lewis came to Australia not on the First Fleet, but on the *Hillsborough* in 1799, after being convicted before a London jury of stealing 56 yards of printed cotton. He offended further when he arrived in the new colony as a convict, and was sentenced to 56 lashes. He then offended again by stealing a boat. James Lewis went on to become one of the 22 male convicts who accompanied Lieutenant Bowen in the first British settlement in Tasmania in 1804. He distinguished himself by being the only person who managed to stage a successful escape from this remote first landing, but was eventually caught and flogged and taken back to Sydney. If my friend, and occasional sparring partner in the ministerial days, Tasmanian Aboriginal activist Michael Mansell had known of my colonial heritage, he could well have charged my convict ancestor with having been part of the 'invading forces' who first helped take the land of Tasmanian Aboriginal people. I wouldn't have been able to deny the charge. At least Michael never found out while I was in that job, as I suspect he would never have stopped gently taunting me about my family history.

Years later, James Lewis gained his liberty and had some free time in the colony before his death. He had only one child, Sarah, who is mentioned in the famous Tasmanian diaries of Reverend Robert Knopwood. Sarah Lewis was born in Sydney in 1802, although there is also some suggestion that she was born on a ship off the coast of Tasmania. She eventually married a convict, Thomas Watkins, and together they operated a hotel somewhere near the corner of what is now Sussex and Druitt Streets in Sydney in the 1820s. In 1838, they moved to the bush and established a farm on the banks of Mangrove Creek, a tributary of the Hawkesbury River. Members of the Watkins family continue to live in this region to this day, and my own grandmother was closely connected with the place as a child. Sarah and her husband are buried on the bank of Mangrove Creek, and recently, in 2016, I paddled my kayak down the creek and scrambled through the mangroves to visit their graves.

My ancestors on my grandmother's side also include convict John Cross, who arrived on the ship *Alexander* in 1788, part of the First Fleet, and commanded by Captain Arthur Phillip. (Observant readers will note that this was, incredibly, the same ship that my mother Gwen's ancestor Andrew Fishburn arrived on.) John Cross married Mary Davidson, who also arrived as a convict, but on the Second Fleet. In the early 1830s, one of John Cross's sons, David Cross, built the Queen Victoria Inn on the banks of the MacDonald River, another tributary of the Hawkesbury, which branches off right at the little township of Wisemans Ferry. While the building is still standing, it is no longer a licensed premises and is now in private ownership. David Cross became the operator of the Wiseman's Ferry after Solomon Wiseman, when it came into government ownership. I understand that Wiseman was the direct ancestor of author Kate Grenville, and the subject of her novel *The Secret River*.

Over recent years, I have often reflected deeply on the potential roles of my ancestors in the killing, dispossession, or further marginalisation of the Aboriginal people of the region during the early 1800s. Ultimately, I have only been able to guess at what those relationships may have been, but it has certainly made me doubly pleased that I have devoted much of my life's work to fighting for the human rights of the Aboriginal and Torres Strait Islander people of this country.

Despite my father's very best efforts to educate me, I am still befuddled by the family history on my father's father's side. I know that it stems from the Scottish heritage of my grandfather William Archibald Murray, who was born in New Zealand and moved to Australia as a young man. His uncle, also named William Archibald Murray, was a member of the New Zealand parliament in the 1800s and apparently one of the leaders of conservative thought in New Zealand politics at the time. I am also related to Bill Hamilton, the New Zealand inventor of the jet boat. Another descendant of the New Zealand Murrays was my grandfather's cousin Sir Angus Murray, who was knighted for his services to gynaecology, and was president of the British Medical Association in Australia (the precursor to the AMA).

Although I didn't know it at the time, and nor did my father, the grandson of Sir Angus Murray is Rob Oakeshott, who became the independent member for Lyne on the north coast of New South Wales after I had left the parliament. My brother Neil heard Rob's first speech in the House of Representatives on the radio and worked out that we're all related. Rob and I have a lot in common, both having chaired the Joint Standing Committee of Public Accounts, as well as the Amnesty International Parliamentary Group. Both of us have a commitment to advancing Aboriginal and Torres Strait Islander rights and a commitment to social justice more generally. It is also a strange irony that Rob represented the electorate of Lyne, which is where I grew up, and which was the seat my father Bert wanted me to represent.

As for the family history on my mother's side, my mother Maida also had a very active interest in discovering that history, and she shared her research with me. There are filing cabinets of family-history research gathered by her, and I'm hoping to bring it all together when I can get the time. She managed to trace her father's side back to colonial English convict roots, with connections to Tasmania as well as the goldfields of Victoria.

Maida was particularly devoted to her own mother, Annie Mary Beasley (nee Killeen), a soft and gentle woman, who had been lived a very hard life, starting off as an orphan. Being so close to someone who had clearly suffered as a result of not having their parents may well have partly informed Maida's grief surrounding my forced adoption, but I can only speculate, as she never mentioned it herself. Maida and Cyn worked assiduously to find out my grandmother's history and heritage. They were able to confirm that she was born in Victoria, the illegitimate daughter of an Irishman, Patrick Killeen. She was later made a ward of the state, and, sadly, Maida and Cyn were unable to further trace her origins.

My maternal grandfather's Beasley side of the family was descended from a convict, James William Beasley (Beezley), who arrived in Tasmania in 1844 on the convict ship *Equestrian*. My grandfather's family had a long association with Orange, and the Beasley name is on the Boer War and World War I memorials in the centre of the town. My grandfather's brother died on the first day of the landing at Gallipoli. I later had the privilege of visiting Lone Pine at Gallipoli and seeing the name of Private W.R.C. Beasley on the memorial there. I was also able to pay him the tribute, with my cousins Gary and Julie, of laying a wreath in his memory at the Orange memorial on the Anzac centenary in 2015. At that time, I was still the CEO of Australian Red Cross, and the local newspaper recounted the fact that the news of my great-uncle's death was sent to the family in Orange in 1916 by Red Cross.

During the roller-coaster of my adoption reunion, I constantly reflected on the wider nature and nurture argument. I'd thought I had it all figured out before I met my birth family. I was sure my personality and core behaviours were a direct product of the upbringing and parenting skills of my beloved adoptive mother and father, Gwen and Bert Tickner, shaped by their respective influences and the powerful influence of the community I grew up in. I still think this view has an undeniable element of truth to it. That is why I have always so passionately fought for social justice and investment in education and communities — to give all children the opportunity to advance their lives. Surely that is the human right of every child in the world.

But then, on meeting my birth parents and my brothers and sisters, the question of what had shaped me became far more complex for me. Things about my own life I thought I'd figured out with absolute clarity and certainty became greyer and more ambivalent.

What I learnt of my family history, particularly the knowledge of those strong political connections in my extended family have, of course, caused me to speculate further on what drove my passionate interests both in politics and in helping to build a better world. Of course, in one of his first letters to me, my father told me what his New Zealand cousins had told him: 'our ancestors for about 600 years have been farmers, doctors and lawyers as well as politicians'. And this was before he had any idea that I was a member of the national parliament.

The truth is, though, I have never thought of myself as a politician; I have always been cause- and conviction-driven, rather than being career-driven. Most of my life I have spent working in the not-for-profit sector and in championing social reform through community-based NGOs and outside political party processes. I remember that even while I was still at school, I was writing letters to the local newspaper, *The Cape Hawke Advocate*, about the government neglect of local roads, which I believed had contributed to the deaths of some of my contemporaries in the town. At high school, I was also writing in opposition to nuclear weapons and as a champion of peace when I wrote in the local RSL Anzac essay competitions. So I can say that, even as a kid, I was a fighter for justice and the causes I believed in.

I was also, as long as I can remember, someone who deplored racial discrimination. I remember as a young schoolboy being very distressed when I visited the local cemetery and found that the graves of local Aboriginal people were relegated to the very back of the cemetery, and often without headstones. Many graves were not identified, and, of those that were, many were marked only with flimsy and transient wooden crosses. Even in death, I saw their poverty and the discrimination against them. My mother Gwen and father Bert are now buried in that cemetery, and I go there often. These days I see a transformation in the way the Aboriginal graves are respected and commemorated: the stories of so many local Aboriginal heroes are now told and recorded in that cemetery. It is a privilege to walk among them and pay respects.

At home, neither my mother Gwen nor my father Bert articulated political views to me of any kind, despite the fact that I later learnt that my father was a card-carrying member of the National Party. My father's newspaper of choice was *The Daily Telegraph*, and it was not known for its championing of social issues. Nor was there anyone in my circle of friends or acquaintances who felt as strongly as I did about issues of social justice. So where did it come from?

Did it, perhaps, come from the sensitive and caring approach to people and life that I saw in my adopted mother, Gwen? Or was it the 'feisty gene' that I inherited from my birth mother, Maida, or an 'empathy gene' that I inherited from my birth father, Len?

That question of nature came up particularly powerfully when I learnt more about my father. In his first letters to me, he revealed his long-term interest in public speaking and his participation in the Rostrum organisation. He had also studied law as a young man, and he had resumed those studies and was enrolled in a law degree when I met him. But deeper than this, I sensed a core dimension of my father's character to be similar to one I saw in myself — a dimension that I knew had been one of the drivers of much of my life's work and my relationships with people. In one of my early letters to him, I mentioned a characteristic of mine 'which some consider a fault, but I can't change. It is that I am very soft. I just can't stand to see people hurting. I have an innate sense of compassion and justice which has influenced my life.' I was baring my soul to my father, and hoped that the intensity of my words wouldn't scare him off. But I came to see that these innate feelings of compassion and love of people were very much part of my father's persona, too, and underpinned all his relationships. It was in this sense that getting to know my father, first through his writing and then in person, was truly the missing dimension in my life.

From my mother Maida, I'm sure I inherited my high levels of energy and spontaneity, which are every bit as important to the heart of my identity. She was a highly intelligent woman, who could have done so many more things in her life had she had the opportunity. She had such core integrity, strength, and determination that if I had inherited half of it, I could have moved mountains.

The end result, though, is that I don't know if I have an answer to the nature-nurture question, or at least not one that makes any sense — I just don't think it's possible to unravel these competing and complementary forces. Modern science and psychological theory accept the same view, I think: that it is not possible to separate or disentangle the forces of nature and nurture, which interact with one another in such complex ways. I am a combination of my genes and my whole life's-worth of experiences, which is the same for everyone. It is one of the delightful and beautiful mysteries of life.

20

Conclusion

My mother Maida's funeral in June 2012 was small, but especially moving for all those present who knew of our family reunion story. She had passed away in the nursing home, after suffering greatly from the ravages of dementia, and Greg had phoned me most distressed to tell me the news. He had been devoted to her in every way. Each day he had driven to the nursing home to hand-feed her and to stay with her throughout the course of the day. At her funeral, family and friends crowded into a little chapel at the crematorium at Pinegrove in western Sydney. I gave the eulogy. I was particularly moved that Sandra, who had played such a huge part in bringing us together, was there that day, too. Her ongoing dedication to my mother was so strong.

In the eulogy, I spoke about my mother's life growing up in Orange — without, of course, mentioning anything of my birth — and I shared how deeply Maida and Greg had engaged with the children of the wider Kirwan and Beasley families. I also spoke about how warmly Maida and Greg welcomed me into their lives, and how they had become the instant and devoted grandparents of Jack. 'I regard my mother as a wonderful life model and a real hero. I respect the deep courage and integrity she displayed in her life, and the abiding love she felt for me, which was deeply reciprocated.'

The headstone we prepared for mother Maida had Greg's and my names on it, and the death certificate that was issued a month later had 'Robert' in the column for 'children'.

After my mother passed away, I found snippets of notes that revealed her state of mind in the immediate aftermath of our adoption reunion. One, I think, was copied from a booklet the Post Adoption Resource Centre had given her: '... but when the grief remains unresolved it can be activated by reunion, setting off the mourning that should have taken place years earlier'.

I can only imagine the turmoil my mother must have gone through at this time, as her grief caught up with her. For 40 years, she had carried the pain and unspeakable guilt of having relinquished me for adoption. None of her friends or workmates knew anything about the birth of her child. She had held this secret so tightly over so many years.

In 2015, I was privileged to read an account of Greg's life story, which he had typed up some 15 years previously. In it, he recorded the circumstances of his meeting up again with Maida when he moved from Orange to Sydney to live (in the years after I was born), and he related the 'shambles and near disaster' of that meeting.

I contacted Maida Beasley and arranged to meet her at Marrickville Railway Station, the suburb where she was boarding at the time. I went down to the station to meet her when I became aware of the loud clanging of a bell emanating from a tram trying to get past this utility parked on the side of the road blocking its progress. Of course, it happened to be my utility, and so I had to shamefacedly repair from the scene much to the ire of the tram driver and its passengers.

In the meantime, Maida, probably suffering from nerves, had to repair to her lodgings nearby to relieve an urgent need. Eventually we did greet one another. This was not a terrific introduction to my first meeting with Maida in Sydney. She must not have been very impressed. Who could this country bumpkin be?

Still the acquaintance grew and there were other meetings, and for my part I became very attracted to this girl. I cannot say that the relationship was a smooth one for there was a lot of on and off occasions.

There was another aspect to overcome. In our talks I learnt that she had some personal trauma at some stage which affected her deeply and was probably the source of a reluctance to be involved in another relationship. I was to learn of her courage shown then and at later times.

That conversation with Greg about my birth and adoption was to sustain my mother for the next 40 years. They never talked about it again.

When I cleaned out my mother's house, long after she had passed away and Greg had moved to an aged-care complex,

I found that, in 1995, she had applied for her and my records from the Crown Street Hospital where I was born, but in secret — such a private person was my mother, and so damaged was she by the time she spent in that hospital and its aftermath. I deeply regret that she chose not to share her pain with anyone, including Greg or me, but that is just how it was for her. The hospital records were forwarded to her on 22 May 1995, and the covering letter reminded her that support and counselling services were available from the Post Adoption Resource Centre. I don't believe she ever took up that offer.

The records show that my mother was admitted to the hospital on 28 November 1951 after being an outpatient. She was 37 weeks pregnant at the time and 22 years old. She spent her birthday — 9 December — in that hospital, and was 23 by the time I was born on 24 December, after she had spent eight hours and 38 minutes in labour.

Among the records, there's a signed consent form for medical procedures that states, 'This is to certify that I have given my consent to have myself operated on or whatever treatment is considered necessary by doctors, under general anaesthetic.' The space on the form for Maida's next of kin was left blank, and I am reminded again how courageous my mother was to embark upon this birth largely on her own.

The records also include a photocopy of an 'adoption card', dated 24 December 1951 (the day of my birth), which states the baby's name as 'D Beasley'. There is another notation on this very small card that refers to 'Social history findings', with the outcome, 'Satisfactory'. The adoption was approved by a doctor, and the 'Infants chart' states that I was born at 1.25 am, weighed 7 pounds 12 ounces, and was 22 inches long.

There are other extensive records concerning my mother, noting what she ate and of course the drugs she was given, but they're written in undecipherable handwriting.

Another form, headed 'Medical examination on discharge', shows that I was discharged from hospital on 11 January 1952, and states that I'd been 'bottle fed' and weighed 7 pounds 11 ounces. Although the form doesn't disclose this detail, I know I was collected that day by my new mother and father, Gwen and Bert Tickner, and taken to 18 Lansdowne Street, Merrylands.

My original birth certificate — which neither my mother nor I saw until over 40 years later — was witnessed by a Doctor Nicholson and a Sister Palmer on 10 January 1952. My new parents were issued with a new birth certificate for me on 8 May 1952, after the completion of all the adoption procedures.

Also interesting to me is the fact that one of the records shows my mother's address as the Tresillian Home in Willoughby, Sydney, although my birth certificate shows her address as 331 Stacey Street, Bankstown. Another hospital form has my mother's family address in Orange, but it's been crossed out and replaced with the address of the Tresillian Home. Perhaps my mother moved from Stacey Street to the Tresillian Home before my birth.

What these records do not show is how my mother felt, alone in this big Sydney hospital, without any real support, as events unfolded around her over which she had little or no control.

In early 2016, Greg's financial circumstances finally required the sale of his and Maida's home at 38 Lansdowne Street, where they had lived for all those decades. The sale also sadly severed my own connection with Lansdowne Street, which had played such an important part in my life since I was taken there as a two-week-old baby in January of 1952. My adopted grandmother's and aunt's houses had both long since been sold.

It took weeks to clear Greg's house, and I kept coming across precious memories in so many of the cabinets and cupboards. There was one find that I nearly missed, as it was concealed at the back of the very top shelf of Maida and Greg's bedroom cupboard. This secreted and tightly guarded document knocked me for six.

Maida had written down her recollection of the circumstances leading to our first meeting in 1993 on the steps of the Sydney Opera House, and her deepest feelings about our reunion. I remembered encouraging her to do this, just as I had done, but obviously the emotions were still so raw for her that she hadn't shared it with me. I don't know for sure, but I am almost certain that she hadn't shared it with Greg, either.

For me, my mother's words are just the tip of the iceberg of the grief that consumed her following my adoption. To me, they represent the grief and pain felt by all relinquishing mothers and their children. There were many tens of thousands of people whose lives were, and continue to be,

affected by the laws and government policies of that time —
laws that were fundamentally flawed. In my mother's case,
the pain lasted a lifetime and left her unable to have further
children because of the all-consuming fear that she would
lose them as she had lost her first.

Our adoption reunion was a turning point in my mother's
life, as her words below make clear, and we became integral
to each other's lives for the next 20 years. Finally, my mother
was able to experience love, peace, and contentment.

*On Tuesday 22nd December 1992, on arriving home from
work my husband Greg asked me if I knew a Sandra. He
said she rang and he told her I'd be home at about 6.30. My
reply was that I could not place a Sandra and if she wanted
me she would ring again.*

*Then I saw a letter for me which I commenced to open. I
KNEW.*

*Immediately went to the bedroom and sat down before
commencing to read the letter. Felt I was in another world.
After some minutes, gathered my thoughts together and knew
I had to privately ring Sandra before 6.30 pm. Remembered
seeing Mrs Hunt* [next-door neighbour] *on her front
verandah seat and, trying desperately to control myself, asked
if I could use her phone.*

*Sandra's voice was so gentle and she asked me if I knew
why she had asked me to ring. I said yes. Sandra explained
that the person concerned wanted to contact me. Sandra
talked; I cried. Sandra mentioned the person was a public
figure. She wanted me to understand that he was a well-*

known person and very much wanted to make contact. She then asked if I was surprised about the public figure and I said quietly, 'No, not really'. Asked Sandra who the person was and she seemed hesitant so I asked again. Sandra told me, but at that stage could not place the person. Do not know at what stage the name and face began to connect in my mind.

After leaving next door, went for a slow half-hour walk.

On arriving back home, sat at the table to eat my cold meal when Greg asked me where I had been. Managed to pick up a knife and fork before the floodgate opened.

At 12 noon on Wednesday 23rd December 1992 arrived at the Ferguson Centre Adoption office, Community Services. Very weepy. Sandra and I talked for two hours then Sandra gave me a letter from HIM and a photo of HIM and his wife and first new baby. A traumatic moment. It was a beautiful letter and beautiful photo. Felt so proud and honoured.

Robert suggested that perhaps I may like to make contact with him on his 41st birthday on 24th December and enclosed his fax and phone numbers. I was emotional and overwhelmed. At 5 am on 24th made up my mind to contact him on his birthday, but not by phone. Could not cope with hearing his voice. As I was not sure where HE was I rang his office in Sutherland to find out if he could receive a fax. My message was ROBERT, HAPPY BIRTHDAY. MAIDA. Later when told I had revealed where I worked [Parramatta City Council letterhead on the fax] I wished the earth would open up and swallow me. How could I be so stupid?

EASY!!! Robert's comment was that I would not make a good spy.

After Christmas I replied to Robert's letter and enclosed three photos of myself. As a 15 year old girl, one taken at Cyn's wedding and one of me holding Jessica [niece] *in Angel Place. In my letter requested a photo of Robert showing his whole face.*

All mail between Robert and myself went through Sandra due to the veto we had both placed with Community Services.

Robert's next letter was 22 pages and enclosing 25 photos with expansions written on the back of each photo. Was able to see the face of Robert, Jody, Jade and baby Jack. What a wonderful moment. Jade at Robert's request made eight pages of writing paper as Robert wanted this to be a family affair. Must add Robert's writing leaves a lot to be desired. His teachers told him this was to cover up for his spelling errors.

On the back of one photo Robert gave the address of his grandmother in Lansdowne Street. Greg bought our land at 38 Lansdowne Street in 1955 and commenced to build. Each weekend I visited Greg to help him. We were married in August 1957 and lived at that address. One great shock was to learn that Robert's grandmother had lived at 18 Lansdowne Street and that two of his aunties lived at 6 Lansdowne Street and 9 Carhullen Street, Merrylands. In the intervening years I wondered how many times I passed this house NOT KNOWING, NOT DREAMING.

Found out later the information of Robert first meeting

Jody as a baby at 18 Lansdowne Street [in 1960]. *What a coincidence — unbelievable.*

From the time of first contact with Sandra to Robert's 22 page letter was a period of about three weeks and during this time I found it very hard to concentrate at work and my eyes were often moist. Also sleeping badly, only for a few hours per night. Saw Robert a few times on TV as the Aboriginal Minister and heard him interviewed by Owen Delaney on radio. Greg taped and videoed Robert's interviews, so I would ask Greg to replay and replay each of them each night. I never really heard what Robert said as I was too occupied searching his face.

Thursday 14th January Robert had an interview with Sandra. Hurried home as the thought of both of us being in Parramatta at the same time was most distressing. At home that night, again studied the photos Robert had sent me. Suddenly looked up and he was being interviewed on TV. Felt like being in a trance and thought, THAT MAN ON TV AND THAT MAN IN THE PHOTOS IS SUPPOSED TO BE CONNECTED TO ME BUT HE IS NOT. I DO NOT KNOW HIM. Suddenly became very distressed and agitated and realised it was because I had NEVER touched him. My pain at that moment was almost unbearable.

Later that night I experienced such peace and calm. I had made my decision and accepted the situation, to proceed forward. Rang Sandra 9 am Friday 15th and said we must meet. Sandra then said Robert cancelled an appointment on Thursday and would be coming into Sydney that afternoon and she should tell me when he arrived. Sandra rang about 4.40 pm on Friday and said, 'GUESS WHO IS IN MY OFFICE'. The tears flowed. So close and yet so far away. Robert had also brought in some lovely flowers from his own garden and these I picked up from Sandra after work and after Robert had left. What a beautiful gesture.

The first convenient day Robert had was Wednesday 20th January so it was arranged we meet at the Opera House Steps at 11 am.

Left home at 9 am and arrived in town at 10 am. Spent half an hour watching the water service scoop up rubbish near Circular Quay. Sometimes I watched people coming and going and wondered who they were meeting. Felt my feet were not on the ground. I was being propelled by destiny. Not afraid of meeting Robert, only nervous.

Walked slowly towards the steps and on the way saw a poor innocent man sitting on a seat by himself. Finally decided it was not Robert spying on me.

Arrived at the Opera House steps a few minutes to eleven. Looked quietly around and thought, HE'S NOT HERE YET. God, don't tell me he's sitting on a seat over there watching me. TERROR.

I looked up and saw a tall dark-haired man waving to me, pointing to himself and calling out, 'IT'S ME, IT'S ME'. It took a few seconds to register it was Robert. Took one step up to him as he hurried down and hugged me. Finally I said, 'I WANT TO SEE YOUR FACE'. He pulled his head back and said in such a voice, 'HERE I AM'. OH OH!

One thing which made me laugh later was Robert

hurrying down the steps calling out, 'IT'S ME, IT'S ME!'
A lady was somehow between Robert and me. She kept
looking at Robert as he descended towards her. Suddenly she
looked down and saw me and very quickly removed herself
from the scene.

It is now twelve months down the track and it has been
a wondrous year.

I am so proud of my beloved son Robert. I can never find
words to express what is in my heart.

Through all the tears, uncertainty, roller-coaster of
emotions and sleepless nights, my dear husband Greg has
always been there for me. So patient, understanding and
positive.

My heartfelt appreciation also goes to our friend Sandra.
Sandra's gentleness, warmth and dedication made it all
happen.

So many caring people have played a part in this story.
Jody, Jade, Jack and my dear family.

MY HEART IS FULL.

BEAUTIFUL MIRACLES DO HAPPEN.

Acknowledgements

Despite the changes in the law in New South Wales and other states allowing adoption reunions to occur, many women and their adopted children continued to suffer greatly, and for so many years the injustices they had experienced remained hidden and the hurt continued. I want to acknowledge here the incredible courage and legacy of the women whose political actions and lobbying persuaded governments to conduct public inquiries and investigations into past adoption practices, and to hold people and institutions accountable for what happened to tens of thousands of Australian women and their children. As a result of these investigations, all Australian governments, including the national government, made formal apologies for those past practices. For thousands of surviving mothers in particular, these actions were welcomed and applauded as setting the historical record straight. Without these women and their achievements, a terrible injustice would have gone unacknowledged. I salute them all.

I also want to acknowledge and applaud the courage and tenacity of those many women and their supporters who campaigned for so long for the reform of the adoption laws in Australia, which gave rise to adoption reunions such as the one I was privileged to experience. They were able to secure the cross-party support of the New South Wales parliament to achieve this law reform: a wonderful achievement.

The clever management of my own reunion is a testimony to the wisdom of all those who had a hand in the preparation of the adoption legislation that made it possible. I particularly want to pay tribute to the past work of the New South Wales Legislative Council Standing Committee on Social Issues, chaired by Ann Symonds, MLC, which, in 1988, began an inquiry into the issue of access to adoption legislation. This all-party committee recommended changes to the law, which were subsequently implemented, and which enabled me to meet my birth families. For that, I am forever grateful.

I shared drafts of this book with a wide range of family and friends, and I thank them all for their advice, encouragement, and wise counsel. In addition to family members, this includes the following people: Olga Havnen, Linda Kelly, Graham Cochrane, Jill Hill, Michael Raper, Diane Hudson, Michael Refshauge, Anne Ditton, Alison Dryer, Marjorie Newman, Norman Grant, Terry Holstein, and Christine Logan.

To my publisher Scribe Publications, so wonderfully led by the renowned Henry Rosenbloom, I owe a particular debt of gratitude for believing that this adoption reunion story was worth telling. I thank Anna Thwaites for her editorial advice and professional final edits of the manuscript.

My friend Nicola O'Shea helped with earlier insightful and invaluable structural advice and undertook a preliminary edit of the manuscript, and I am so grateful for her work.

Anne Newman was a constant source of forthright advice and encouragement, and I could not have written this book without her.

Finally, I want to thank my family for allowing me to tell this story.

Balmain, August 2019